WRITERS REPUBLIC

DAMAGED
"BUT GOD"

CHARLES DEAN BOWSER

Copyright © 2022 by Charles Dean Bowser.

All rights reserved. No part of this book may be reproduced in any form or by any electronic or mechanical means, including information storage and retrieval systems, without permission in writing from the publisher, except by reviewers, who may quote brief passages in a review.

This publication contains the opinions and ideas of its author. It is intended to provide helpful and informative material on the subjects addressed in the publication. The author and publisher specifically disclaim all responsibility for any liability, loss, or risk, personal or otherwise, which is incurred as a consequence, directly or indirectly, of the use and application of any of the contents of this book.

WRITERS REPUBLIC L.L.C.
515 Summit Ave. Unit R1
Union City, NJ 07087, USA

Website: *www.writersrepublic.com*
Hotline: *1-877-656-6838*
Email: *info@writersrepublic.com*

Ordering Information:
Quantity sales. Special discounts are available on quantity purchases by corporations, associations, and others. For details, contact the publisher at the address above.

Library of Congress Control Number: 2022922027
ISBN-13:   979-8-88810-230-5   [Paperback Edition]
                 979-8-88810-231-2   [Digital Edition]

Rev. date: 12/28/2022

Introduction

Damaged "But God"

Please understand that my intentions are not to air out my family's history with disrespect nor for amusement to bring out regrets and shame but to allow the world to see from my point of view of how the power of God made a difference in my life and in my family. There was a time in my life that I had to choose either to be what I've always been and stay confined in my prison or trust God and for many years I chose prison over everything and in doing so everyone of my family members suffered from the damage that surrounded me.

As I sit here and tell the story of how God made away in my life and spared me from death many times. I want the world to know through my struggles and trials and all the damage that I created only God could have seen me through it all. I hope and pray that my words become a platform of what's to come for those who takes pleasure in pressing on throughout adversity, for had it not been for God's unchanging hands I don't know where I would be. Unlike many reality shows, my life story is far from a show. It's the ups and downs of a damage childhood and an even more damage adult life full of abandonment, mental health issues, crime, peer pressure, drugs and an addictive personality that gives me the strength and courage to reveal what it took for my life to change.

But Gods grace and mercy surely outweighed myself destructive patterns that ultimately led me in prison and many times knocking on deaths door. It's not unusual to see in every neighborhood there are many families like my own. Through the strength of God I pray that my story uplift's and bring awareness to those who are struggling with depression, addiction and suicidal thoughts. I have tried so many times to make my will be the Lords will only to be blinded by the Holy Spirit. I say that with deep admiration. When we lose our view, we see the shining light of Gods mercy and his forever promise that he will never leave us in his many miracles that surrounds us daily Hallelujah! Although for many years I looked at my life as a failure. Along with that came DAMAGE. Whether it was DAMAGE I brought on to others and or the self-DAMAGE I bestowed upon myself.

I realize that many will relate too and be familiar with each chapter of my life. Yet the main ideal in each message is "BUT GOD". Over and over again I can't express it enough just what "BUT GOD" truly means to me and acknowledging his continuous care for me and my family in moments when we didn't't care for ourselves. My self-worth was indeed the force of all my reasons to take life and others for granted.

I can view my life with this phrase in mind, like a crystal ball you get to see the future and you notice short comings that seem to be within reach to change the outcome of your cause and effect. You have the power to change it but because of your own ignorance you are left to believe that there has to be a glitch in what you are seeing, this can't be happening to me and in our thoughts, we blink so it doesn't affect us but it does .When you least expect it you can lose your view and your way. In just that moment when you take for granted life it can be for bad or good and or damaged either way "BUT GOD" is the only way for correction. And through it all we must understand that he has power remarkable power that can change our course in life only if we lean on him. It may have taken me a lifetime to get that in my head yet I'm so glad I know now God's gift to me is to allow the world to see that it's never too late to trust in his grace.

Damaged "But God"

Chapter 1

The Family

I was born on December 22, 1965, in Kansas City, Kansas. My mother, Geraldine, and my father, Charles, had three boys: Carl, the oldest; Kenny, the middle; and me, Charles, the baby. We grew up mainly in the projects on Second Street in Jupiter Gardens. Many families that resided there were either low income or no income meaning poor.

In the beginning of me understanding the reality of my life, I realized at a very early age that my mom acted as both mother and father in our home. Mainly because my father was in and out of prison. I found out later that he was doing the only thing he knew how although in the beginning he had several jobs but because of my mother's high demands and his willingness to please her and provide for his family he chose crime to be the more easier way to satisfy us all. He was a very strong man but heartless when it comes to family values and decisions making. Even today, years after his passing, I still don't recall him ever telling myself or my brothers, "I'm proud of you!"

In the projects, it appeared that there were no fathers in any family and as time went on, the children of the projects protected each other with all types of false comfort and most of us had no true understanding of what a family truly looked like.

My mother, on the other hand was strict but consistent. A God-fearing woman that comes from a family of thirteen children with her being the twelfth child. Even though she was one of the youngest and given the least amount of attention she had to learn on her own what love really meant. When her parents got sick she made it her duty to be there for them both until God called them home. Because of that unemotional bond and the lack of moral family support as a child she overlooked her childhood and took on the responsibility as a young mother and raised her boys herself. Through all the ups and downs she kept her faith in the Lord for godliness.

As the projects knew of The Bowser Boys, we were hard to deal with. We grew up at the beginning with not a lot so my mom taught us how to appreciate what we did have and with all the confusion with growing up without a father in the home my mother kept us in church in hope that we wouldn't be easily influenced in the streets.

We grew up under the guidance of Reverend David L. Gray, the only father figure of many families in those days. We all attended Pleasant Green Baptist Church on Sundays, Tuesdays, Wednesday, and Saturday. Even now I'm smiling because on revivals we attended seven days straight. I guess you can figure out how important it was to my mother to make God and attending church a priority.

Although at times Pastor Gray and most of the mothers would have to come to retrieve many of us children from the basketball courts of Gateway projects because we would go there immediately after Sunday school. They would march us all to the front of church just to prove a point that they were in control and no matter what they had their eyes on us. Let's not get ahead of ourselves for Gateway was an important part of my life that I must give more than a mention of because that's where the excitement happened especially on Sunday on the basketball court. Gateway was the cornerstone to 5th street where anything goes if you weren't on the concrete playground playing ball or just chilling then you were watching all the crazy activities unfold on the strip.

Going back to my mother in the early years we really struggled not having our father around so when my mother got her a job she worked her butt off just to make sure we had the best. She worked for Hallmark Cards for thirteen years along with many other just to provide for our family. Due to her work schedule, my oldest brother, Carl, became a big brother and father figure to us all. My mother was so much fun at the beginning yet at times demanding like an Army Sergeant. I remember one of the things she use to always say: "This is going to hurt me more than it's going to hurt you." Wow, it took almost thirty years for me to understand exactly what that message meant, realizing after having my own children that it would kill me to discipline them. But I realized it had to happen in order to correct their bad behavior and habits.

Now trust me, the Bowser Boys received more than their fair share of beatings or what my mom called it being disciplined. As bad as it sounds, that's what brought us boys closer than ever. Most of the time, we all got punished for something that the other brother did, but we refused to tell on each other. It didn't matter what it was in our eyes my mom was the enemy and she got on us for everything. There was a time where the ice box was left open and keep in mind it could have been by accident but because she was so brutal with her attack and honestly she probably was the one who did it but we all got in trouble yet we just kept quiet and took the punishment. It seemed like this went on forever and I think it was just an unspoken knowledge that if given a chance to get away from her and that house we wouldn't hesitate at any means necessary.

I remember that every Christmas I would be sick. Once I realized I was allergic to walnuts, I ate as many as I could so I would get sick. Mainly because my mother would celebrate my birthday on Christmas and that meant that I wouldn't be celebrating both but just one. So on purpose to gain some extra attention from her, which rarely happened I would get sick lol. But the only one that gave me extra attention was Carl. Carl would come play with me especially during that time while I was sick but later on in the years I realized that was his job to keep me safe. That's what made Carl so important in my life because he was always there.

After my father went to prison my mother later on had a daughter with her boyfriend Sam. My sister Samantha was born when I was almost four years old in 1969. Let me add: my mother did not introduced many men in our lives at all. This turned out to be one of the first major life changing experiences in our lives.

Us boys watched our mother get into a physical altercation with Sam that led to her being hospitalized. Talk about change of dynamics. That situation made me full of fear and hate and it began the trauma that lead me to isolate. Carl and Kenny became so hardened over what happened to our mother that they vowed to never show their emotions toward others ever again and that meant rage would protect them when they didn't understand what they felt.

I can remember sitting on the stairs and hearing my mother cry out as Carl held me in his arms. Kenny just sat there holding his hands in a fist, full of rage. Even to this day, I believe that isolated situation stagnated our growth and development. My mother made it through her traumatic experience and because of her will to live for her children and also her lack of knowledge to abuse, she took Sam back. No matter what we felt about Sam, he continued to provide for us all. The one person that never accepted Sam was Kenny because of that situation.

My sister Samantha was the key to making our family whole again mainly because she was the baby girl that brought so much joy into our lives. And at the time that made sense of why my mother stayed. Adding my baby sister made us boys become more responsible and protective of her. We didn't let her see all the madness and drama that we experienced daily. And she noticed how things had affected her brothers and their inabilities to function in society as she grew up. Due to their escaping their emotional detachment in whatever way they could.

One day Sam had an altercation with Kenny and being that the wounds were never healed from what we witness years before with our Mother, Sam hit Kenny in the head with a belt buckle that open his head with a flood of blood and trust me that caused Kenny to hate Sam for life. After that whenever Sam would try to discipline any of us it just didn't settle at all. Kenny never got over it and from that day he vowed he would repay him for what he had done to him and our mother.

I can remember Kenny was strong and took the blame for almost everything because he just didn't communicate well. He just held everything in, but when he got to a boiling point, he would explode like a tornado and everything around him he would be destroy. Kenny was very quiet and easygoing, he was one of the greatest thinkers I know. When I was born, I looked so much like him that people confused us as twins.

One day we were both outside playing in the backyard. Kenny was six, and I was five and we liked digging in the dirt. He had dug up a very old metal clothes hanger and it hit me in my left eye. It wasn't his fault but the hanger hit me right in my pupil and destroyed my left eye.

My mother was at work and all I can remember after that was laying on a gurney and rolling down the white line at the old KU medical center. I was going straight to surgery and I was hearing my mother cursing at Kenny and him saying, "Mama, I didn't mean it." I woke up in the hospital with a patch on my eye and later had to get the eye removed because if they tried to save it the older I got it would cause more problems especially knowing that the pain would never go away and as a child it was difficult to understand so my mom made the decision to have the eye removed. This accident also changed the course of my life forever. I can remember returning countless times to the hospital and all the laughter from kids because of my patch. One of the most hurtful things they called me was Popeye the Sailor Man. Even though it was a great cartoon, it hurt my feelings deeply because the kids made it sound so mean. And because I didn't and couldn't understand the misfortune of my new defect. I escaped reality with even more fear and isolation.

Carl and Kenny used to fight off all the kids who would make fun of me and seriously I just couldn't understand why they didn't have anything else to do besides causing me so many tears. I can remember my mother buying me Army Men to play with because none of the other kids would play with me. This was something that I could play with by myself that would fulfill my loneliness in my moments of isolation.

Growing up in the projects was hard because in the 1970s, it was all about the concept of robbery, pimping and hustling either way you see it you were taking something by force and or by manipulation. If you were slow then you were slow indeed. Being that everything was fast one had to keep up or stay on the porch. So guess what, I stayed on both porches front and back playing with my Army Men.

Most of the time my mother kept me with her wherever she went so that meant I stayed in the church morning—day and night. While we were growing up our mother made sure we as boys and brothers stuck together and she put that instruction in Carl's head at a very early age. Because I was the youngest Carl's responsibility was mainly to keep up with me. I remember he would be waiting for me after school to pick me up. He would cook and clean up after all of us. Carl was tough and fearless as he watched everything and everyone. The one thing I can remember about Carl growing up was that he put so much on his back, especially his little brothers. No one could tell him he couldn't succeed; he never ran from a challenge even at an early age which made him the backbone of our family.

Carl, Kenny and I all had a certain image to uphold individually. Most of this was gained by lack of emotions; rather it was fear, anger, and aggressiveness. Either way we made it through the early years believing our destiny to be damaged. For we had no other hope but each other. Sports would prove that God gave us a voice to be recognized by—good, bad, or indifferent.

Damaged "But God"

CHAPTER 2

The Bowser Boys

Damaged "But God"

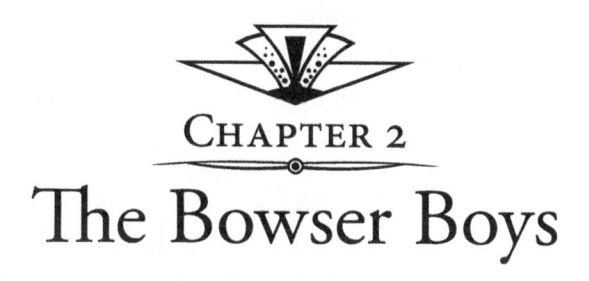

Growing up in the Jupiter Gardens projects was hard, especially if you weren't either criminal minded or sports minded. At a very young age my brothers and I needed an escape from all the pressure at home; and although Carl and Kenny had the God-given gift to be good in sports (some would even say later that they were great in all sports), I on the other hand no matter how hard I tried just didn't measure up to their ability on the gridiron. After many years of just trying to fit in I had to come to terms with the fact that sports just wasn't for me.

Yet for Carl and Kenny they showed and proved to the entire hood that they belonged and their physical power and boldness in every activity they participated in. Not to mention that they never back down from anything especially a fight and or challenges. From Benjamin Banneker to Northeast High School and from Rosedale Middle to JC Harmon, my brother stayed on the front page. Carl and Kenny played every sport so they wouldn't have to go to church every day and night. Like I said, being raised by our mother alone. She kept us grounded in church and made sure we acknowledged Christ Jesus as our Lord and Savior. Carl and Kenny figured out how to use their talents in sports to get out of their daily church involvement; but one thing I can remember is that although they got away from the church function, they didn't get away from the prayer service we had in our home every night. Trust me, I used to think my mom didn't have anyone else to talk too but God cause she would pray for hours and we boys used to be like, "Oh my God, hear her already" (laugh out loud!). Yet later on as we got older we understood what the power of a praying mother meant. My mother prayed about everything and I can remember when all my aunts and uncles would come over and the party would start and my mother would be playing church and other music. Nothing could stop her from praising God listening to whatever it always ended with something about God.

And because I really didn't participate in sports activities she kept me with her in the church. She even had me join the choir. Believe it or not I became a really good singer and I went from church to church singing. At that time I just wanted to make my mom happy. At thirteen I sang at the Emanuel Cleaver's Church. The song was "Wade in the Water." I was so scared yet in the crowd of hundreds I could hear my mother shout out "It's okay baby. Sing to Mama." And I did just that. Hallelujah!

Because of not being an athlete nor truly interested in anything I was left alone not sharing in my brother's competitive sports outings. I was left at home on the porch where I had seen so much drama from the streets that would one day be my rise and fall to temptation like the dice games and most of the pimps and thugs persuasions. It left a huge impression on me. I thought it was such an amazing concept just to be able to be in control with a jazzy conversation. I just wanted to be noticed for something.

I couldn't match my brothers in sports but I was known on the streets at age ten and eleven as a gambler and a street cat that would do almost anything for money. I can remember that at age six I went with my mom to visit my father in the county jail. After leaving I told my mom that I was going where my dad was because I wanted to stay longer visiting with him although at the time I didn't realize it nor knew what I was saying but that set the stage and I mean just those words they changed the course of my life and my destination was set for destruction from that point on. Damaged "But God"

With all the new found fame in the sports world my brothers received a lot of attention and walking to the bus stop every day together was the best moments of my life. Our friends and schoolmates would always say, "There goes the Bowser Boys." They were not really talking about me but because I was there I just made it fit lol. I really didn't know how important or how good my brothers were especially in basketball until we went to the Gateway projects and Carl and Kenny showed up and showed out. It was like an NBA game and I mean anybody who was somebody showed up. My brothers were hard-core and everybody knew who they were. I remember sometimes fights would break out and Carl and Kenny were right in the middle and even though I couldn't fight I would try to act like I was going to do something just in case we had to answer to my mom cause she would be very direct that if you get into a fight and all three of you are there then all three better be involved so you just knew that if you got into it with one of us you had to deal with all of us or deal with moms afterwards. All I ever did was watch my brothers at fifteen and sixteen take on the entire basketball court and we would leave smiling full of energy and the hood knew not to mess with the Bowser Boys. That outlook really damaged our view of the world because it became apparent that no one could tell us nothing.

Carl was tall and lanky but very quick. Ever since I can remember he was the best at whatever he would put his mind to. And being that he was light-skinned it made him that one guy that everybody wanted to be around and with especially the girls and I'm not lying he would have them stop in and out like it was a car wash lol let me make it very clear only when moms was at work cause if she ever found out it would have been hard to explain. Carl was so nice-looking and carried himself in a way that demanded respect. Carl was a good brother. I remember when all the kids would tease me because of the patch I wore on my left eye and how he would always make sure that I didn't feel less than the other kids by letting them know that he was my big brother and trust me that meant so much to me and it carried a lot of weight.

My brothers always made me feel special. Not to mention because Carl and Kenny were so popular I always received a pass for a lot of things I did lol and once again as I grew older I stayed involved in something. Like the time I broke into someone gym locker and stole their shoes and wore them the next day like it was nothing and this big dude noticed that I was wearing his shoes and chased me down the hall until Carl realized it was me running for my life lol by the time I ran behind him he didn't ask no questions just began to beat dude down only to find out that I stole the man's shoes either way I got away with everything. What's so crazy that same day Kenny had to fight off another guy that was on my ass also for something I stole. I was their little brother and it showed. I can even recall it like it was yesterday how I would wait for Carl to come home at nights because he would bring me apple pies from Church's Chicken my favorite. My brothers were a big deal to me. Carl taught me how to shoot dice and the first time I really ever played for money it was against him but I never won because he knew how to cheat. Carl was great with figuring things out especially in sports. Because of his height he was untouchable on the basketball court and on the football field. At J. C. Harmon, Carl walked around like Jordan and became so cocky that as he grew older it became a curse. And because of the sense of entitlement it caused damage to his thinking and later his demise and death.

In 1983, Carl went to Independence Community College on a football scholarship and did a great job at first but soon began to revert to the dysfunctional patterns that he picked up from the streets.

He was such a manipulator that once he got his feet wet in that small town he couldn't resist the freedom it gave him especially since he didn't have much of that growing up his entire life changed and it was apparent that the damage of the past had set in and he gave up on his education and sports career to search out the temptations of the unknown.

One thing the streets does is teach you how to survive and Carl took to it full bloom. From hustling drugs to robberies and with that came his mission to control women. Because he was really handsome it caught the attention of the ladies and not only did he look good but his conversation was top class and easily trapped one's fascination and curiosity. All of this sounds great at the moment but like anything that flies high it has to one day come down especially when the intent is not pure.

In 1985, Carl's gifts of illegal persuasion came to a halt and he was convicted of robbery. While in prison, Wichita State sent him a letter in hopes that if he could make better choices they would give him at least a conversation to see if he wanted to come back to school. Carl understood that his life wasn't over and was determined not to let this setback kill his chance to perform at what he did best. Competing in sports was his dream from day one and he believed that once he got out of prison he would pursue his dream again.

While in prison Carl kept his nose clean and worked on his basketball skills whenever he could. In 1987 he was transferred to Lansing State Prison where I was and I can't tell you really how excited I was to see him cause I hadn't seen Carl in almost two years. Although I was in prison before Carl we were together in Hutchinson until I got into a fight with the guards and was transferred out in 1985. Our reunion was short lived but I was able to get Carl in the cell with me for a few days before he was moved again to the Farm. My mom told me later while on the phone that she talked to Carl and he told her mama I don't know who this person is but it's not my little brother and I got to get away from him cause he ain't trying to come home. Looking back wow I didn't noticed it but I wanted Carl to know and see that I was a man and in control but I just showed him I was institutionalized and in a caged is where I belonged.

In 1988, Carl was released from prison yet all his ambition didn't last long. He returned to the old behaviors and ways of thinking that caused the damage to his own life. In 1989 after being released the first time myself in August me and Carl sold drugs to an undercover agent and although the drugs were mine Carl as he has always done took the rap for his brother. He claimed the drugs were his just to keep me from going back to prison again. He was given seven years.

Damaged "But God"!

While in federal prison Carl was murdered over a basketball game altercation in November 1993.

He said many times that he was tired of defending himself over the game of basketball and all the jealousy from the other inmates. One thing about Carl was he wasn't going to back down from anyone or anything. His pride wouldn't let him do it.

Carl got into a verbal argument with a gang member from a different state over a basketball game which happens a lot because of the betting/

gambling that the inmates did to pass time. That game went from words to a direct threat of violence and from there to a physical fight that didn't end there.

Carl was warned that if he didn't check off the yard he was going to have to face death. My brother was well recognized all over the prison for he was very strong mentally and physically fit. He never involved himself in the bull shit and for sure wasn't a follower and they knew it. Un-afraid of the possibility of death he made it known he wasn't checking in or off the yard no matter what.

My brother has never been scared of the odds for he believed he was a sure thing to win at any level and he would always say bet on me I can't lose, for sure winner especially when his back was against the wall.

Carl was the head of the Bowser Boys and that meant as confusing as it may sound that death was not an option when it came to survival …Carl went to that day room understanding that he wasn't going to be made weak period and at whatever cost they were going to know he was going out fighting. He went to battle only to be surprised for they came as a pack of cowardly dogs and he was all alone and the deck was truly stacked against him. More than what he expected we're waiting on him and the day room door was shut as soon as he entered. Carl gave them all he could and they knew he would, he backed himself against the wall and fought off as many as he could until a chair leg was broken and jammed into his neck. At 6'5 he was a beast and like an animal was taken down and left for dead and after being hit several times the officer's came to his aide but was amazed of the damage that was done.

Carl died a week later.

It's always been about the game with Carl he did it with a smile like it was always so easy for him to shine he lost his life because they feared him and yet fear was never apart of his makeup. There has always been a question in my mind that has never been answered to this date. Why was he alone in that day room? Yet I know my brother he never has depended on cowards they always needed him or teamed up against him.

If I had the opportunity to say anything to my brother although so much grief and pain that has been killing me for so many years. I would say to him Carl I need you to know how much I love you and I thank you for always putting me first in times of adversity I'm so sorry I didn't listen to you when you said you didn't feel right going with me because that was God warning you. Lord knows I wish it was me cause you had so much more to offer this world and I know that doesn't make sense I just wish I would have listened to you for you would be here now and my heart wouldn't hurt every time I breath. I hope no I know you are watching me and I need you to know that my work is far from over cause as long as God gives me strength I will keep your memories as my motivation to win. I've had so much to get through in life and just to get too this level of elevation as God be my witness I use to fear everything about life because you weren't here. Yet when I decided to follow Christ Jesus full heartedly the Bible taught me how to let go and let God and that's when he blessed me with the words and title of this book. And because of you I dedicate it to you.

Forget me not remember I told you that in a poem now its in a book I MISS YOU!!!!

Damaged "But God."

King of all kings Kenny my twin was a gladiator from birth. He took everything on the chin nothing could break him. From a young age he vowed never to do drugs because he witnessed all the damage it caused the people around him. Kenny just like Carl, took sports as a gateway to escape the issues at home and a way to get out of church functions. Kenny was really smart yet the one thing that created most of his dysfunctional experience was his inability to express himself without anger.

Growing up Kenny was an over thinker and when it came time to express what his thoughts and/or emotions were it would cause him to shut down mainly because he just didn't do well with others and he felt that in order for him to protect his self from the world and from being made a fool of that it was easier just to present himself as to be mean and angry all the time. I remember Kenny would take the punishment for me and Carl and

I watched him not shed one tear it didn't matter who was to blame for it cause it became apparent that our mother automatically blamed Kenny. Sometimes I would wonder why he was so angry but I didn't know it than but my brother was suffering from some deep mental shit and he would take those beating without ever telling the truth that it wasn't even him and not just that but in his mind he also felt the need to be the protector in everything he did. Later in life that code would cause him to distance himself because it would become to much of a task that would ultimately break him with shame.

Damaged "But God"

Kenny was so unlike myself and Carl growing up for he just wanted to be left alone and if that meant staying in his room then so be it but there was never a time he would let Carl go anywhere alone and the thing is Carl always was on the go so Kenny stayed even more pissed off lol cause that took him away from his quiet time. Kenny could literally sleep an entire day and still get into trouble unbelievable but true lol.

As time would come later growing up Kenny did venture out into some criminal behaviors he was sneaky enough and got away with it because unlike Carl and myself Kenny wasn't loud and apparent. Kenny on the other hand allowed other people and friends who wanted the lime lights to be the center of attention while he got his dirt in without being noticed. I guessed after taking the blunt of punishment for so many years for me and Carl he decided that the pressure should be put on someone else.

In school Kenny was just as good as if not equal to Carl in all sports he actually played varsity all four years. He was one of the purest shooters I witnessed in those days. My brothers grew up with Calvin "Pony" Thompson one of the greatest basketball player ever to come out of the projects and they would play together all the time. I remember going to the courts at Edginton on 4th street to watch Pony and Carl and Kenny play against the older guys and win a lot. They would go from neighbors competing for the right to be KING of the courts.

Kenny enjoyed the game but was really good in football because he could release so much anger especially when he hit the opposing team. One thing about Kenny: you wouldn't know he was upset with you till he came at you. He just never showed his hand. He and Carl were so competitive that at times it would appear that they didn't even know each other because of how hard they played against each other yet in that position it caused them to rise above any competition.

When Carl left for college in 1983, Kenny used that opportunity to leave the house to go live with his girlfriend. It was his senior year and he really stood out in football and basketball but didn't get many offers that caught his attention more than the marines. Being that he had a family, his son was just born and because of his vow to commit to family values he made the sacrifice to take the sure thing in supporting his family by enlisting into the marines.

Before graduating from high school Kenny spent most of his time away from the house because of his constant struggle with our mom. Kenny was always off to himself and like I mentioned earlier he just didn't get alone with anyone which is so funny cause going to the marines really did put him in immediate contact with others constantly but because of the traumatic experiences as child I guess he hoped for something different in a different world

Kenny was always embarrassed by a lot of the issues we had at home growing up like just the thought of going to the store with food stamps would horrify him and he would be bother by everything some of the kids would say like they use to talk about our shoes cause they were ran over but who cares they still couldn't hold neither one of my brothers on the courts I would always think. And it was even more embarrassing to Kenny to hear the kids call our mom a drunk or whatever it didn't matter lol he would always use something to keep himself mad as if just being raised up in our house wasn't enough.

My brother did have a funny side he was a true comedian he could talk about you so bad that after it was over he would also have to kick your butt because of how he embarrassed you and he would make you feel as though you had to try to defend yourself and if you didn't know you would learn pretty fast that he joked so abusively because it was a form of aggression that he could release and back it up with violence lol and he use every tool he had to push you to the limits in hope that you would want to fight.

One of the many lessons I learned from Kenny was to always take care of your appearance. He would take so much pride in how he dressed and what he looked like that it seemed like he was going to an audition every morning before school and I mean from head to toes always matching and smelling good. There were times I would sneak and wear his clothes and he would somehow find out and haunt me down and literally make me come out of it no matter where I was lol.

My brother was kind to myself and Carl especially to me when I wasn't stealing. I remember I would get into fights and of course I would always get beat up and that happened a lot. On many occasions I can remember for one reason or another losing and it didn't matter who or why I got into the fight everyone around would say afterwards omg here comes Kenny and with that said you knew Superman was coming to save his little brother and I mean it would be brutal for whoever thought they got away with beating me up.

Kenny, I don't know if he really knows but my quest to be a man was always influenced from his example in everything he stood for and the way he lived his life as a father and brother and most definitely as a man. And I say this because with all the damage that has happened around you and all the constant reminders of Carl and myself in our decisions in life, you never became unfocused in becoming the best you. Kenny one thing you taught me was that talk is cheap and I can't continue to live in the past if I plan to succeed in the future.

Being raised by a single mom and struggling with his inability to be recognized as worthy Kenny went through a lot that resulted to him being such a private person. Him and Carl did so much together yet were so much different in the way they responded to personal issues and because my mother was so hard on Kenny for whatever reason it was psychologically it caused him to hold life expectations at arms length and because of all the anger and resentment that he bottled up inside to this date still comes out as pain but I know its always been a cover up so he wouldn't have to feel and its far from funny because the one lesson my mother never taught us was how to feel emotionally cause then you had to be human and in our home well as Kenny seen it we were robots.

And as I write this I can remember Kenny was most definitely feared not for his words but for his actions. Kenny stayed in the marines for over eight years. He escaped most of our lives through isolation and distance rather it be in mind and or body. I never knew his real pain and how he blocked out so much in order to keep from hurting cause he wasn't there for Carl and I as we got older but in the last few years he finally confided in me about our childhood and Carl's death and wow I never knew he hurt so much for so many things in our lives until one day during a visit he just lost it and cried his eyes out. This story is about the pain of three brothers that loved unconditionally and yet still never knew what love was in the eyes of normalcy.

Damaged "But God"

Throughout all my years of trying to find myself and what God's reason for his constant mercy in my life was meant for. I have for many years stopped myself from acknowledging the pain and fear of my sister's tears. I told myself that as long as I protected her from all my drama and destruction it wouldn't personally affect her. Although I experienced my share of failure from my decisions I seriously didn't think it would cause any damage in the lives of my family especially my sister.

Being raised in a church atmosphere and knowing the Lord in all his wonders I believed that no matter what road I took my sister would understand that she had to overcome any obstacles that she encountered. *Damaged "But God"* is also about my baby sister and all that she endured growing up in the Bowser family. And still through it all she never lost her faith in God and what his purpose for her life would be.

It is also to bring awareness to all the women, young and old who had to grow up in a world without the comfort of their brothers because of their decisions that caused them to be incarcerated and or to lose their lives. As a brother I failed to see the impact of my decision in my life that would affect my sister life. It wasn't because I took her for granted I just didn't think emotionally that she would suffer. Although we were very close I believed that she would just go on with her life and know that she had to make better choices in order not to struggle in life. My mom always taught me and my brothers to respect women and always protect our sister and seriously just us not being in her life should have been a blessing cause being there added so much more drama especially with me it was enough pressure just with the embarrassment of all the negative talk of all the drama that I surly brought every time I got into trouble.

I can't go back and change my past but I can express the worth of my sister and my mom and I heard the cry's and stories of a lot of guys in prison wishing they could just say to their sisters and moms I love you. I pray that as you read my story that you know I speak for those that can't speak because of death or life in prison. You are recognized even when we don't say the words just knowing our existences is only made possible because of you a woman and I'm saying this to my sister Samantha it's because of all your prayers and tears that I write this book and have fought hard every day to live a righteous life because I never ever want to leave you alone again. You taught me humbleness and patience and one day I pray you see just how much you really mean to me.

My sister tears and all the unknown fears were always measured by my inability to not to stay out of trouble. Samantha was my best friend growing up because it was always just us. Carl and Kenny would always be going to one event or another enjoying their freedom in sports. We made the best out of being around each other especially when mom was on her alcohol kick.

When Samantha was born our lives was full of confusion because my mom was struggling with drinking and her relationship with my sister dad and not to mention she was trying to manage God in her life as well in ours. It was hard for her trying to keep structure and balance in her boy's lives and she knew she would give her life just to keep them safe at whatever cost and trust me with all the discipline and overbearing down your throat religious threats we felt like she was killing us in a sense cause the force of it all was taking our breath away.

This story is not any different from any story when it relates to growing up in a home with a single mother in the projects with 3 boys and 1 girl trying to maintain their daily activities and working hard every day with no help in this world that was filled with many deception and distractions most times it became overwhelming. Yet those that held on to their faith in God found away to defeat the peer pressure of society and the learned dysfunctional core beliefs that most kid adapt from the false reality of their environment, that I must belong to this or that in order to fit in or to be accepted. And my mother I know today only did what she felt was best for us and most definitely she worked with what she believed to be effective at any cost. Either way growing up in the projects with no true role model is not my full story but it is the beginning of the damage to my entire family.

At a young age Samantha noticed that her life was so much different than most because of the abuse of alcohol in our home by our mom and the pressure of being forced to go to church. She also noticed that her brothers had become distant from the church and home and because of that she dealt with so much tension that she had to endure. Most of the time she was in the house consumed with the chores and cleaning up after mom. She wasn't allowed to do anything outside the house unless it was church related and as she got older she understood why.

Carl and Kenny were always gone so me and Samantha did everything together when I was younger due to an accident I had to learn to get use to using just one eye and because of that I wasn't very comfortable hanging out with the other kids so I spent most of my time playing with army men toys but when I got bored I would expose my energy on upsetting Samantha in anyway I could.

One day as I was being my normal pain in the butt to my sister I went a little too far and as Samantha repeatedly told me to stop playing I continue to nag her and she hit me so hard and before I realized it I was rolling down the stairs in sure agony as she came running she noticed blood everywhere and she stood amazed and stunned. My mom was called from work and I had to be rushed to the hospital and went straight into surgery in hope that it didn't affect my only one good eye.

Samantha was 6 and I was 10. After leaving surgery and coming home from the hospital I was once again ready to play again lol my sister told me didn't you have enough, she said stop and that time I understood she was serious so I listen cause I didn't want no part of her fist again and to be totally clear I hate I had to learn it the hard way that she was nothing to mess with lol.

Growing up with siblings that's what they do. They get into it and then it's all love after the point is made but it's always someone with hurt feelings and a busted eye unfortunately it was me lol yet regardless to what happens at home no one got it confused outside the house that we would die for each other and that's without a doubt.

I remember when I would get spankings for some of the many things that I would do and Samantha would be waiting till it was all over and sneak me food and sweets and most of the time she wouldn't even go outside because she would stay in her room talking and laughing with me. She would also cry for me especially when I would make my punishment worse than it had to be.

When Samantha was young she watched us boys go through our many transitions into our teenage years and adulthood. Each one of us boys had our reasons to hurry up and grow physically and mentally so we could get out of the house and she watched the destruction of my many bad choices and the pain it caused my mother and her.

Being left alone when you are so close to someone is so damaging and I can remember the times when the police would come for me and my sister's face would be so full of tears. Never one single word just a river of tears. Each time I was incarcerated I never thought about whether my sister would be okay because I knew she was the female version of the Bowser Boys because of what she was instilled with.

My mother really kept a close eye on my sister and sometimes that strict love became more of a punishment. Always on her for one thing or another and today I realize why. My mother didn't want Samantha to enhance the distraction in life as my brothers and I did. Tough love is what they call it and it was indeed very tough.

My sister never experienced the streets like we did and I'm sure she was tested with peer pressure and rebellious behaviors but I'm surer of the fact that she didn't want to disappoint my mother.

Like Carl and Kenny, my sister graduated from high school and went to college. She has kept a job her entire life. Even when she became pregnant with her daughter Candace she didn't let that change her commitment to be the best.

Like most young women that are controlled and trapped in the house by an overprotective mother once they get any type of freedom they go straight in and once my sister got pregnant she experienced the lies of a man and realize she wasn't missing anything so she decided to take her daughter Candace and managed her upbringing alone. My sister never needed to be noticed or wanted the attention of many man especially a street dude mainly because they reminded her of her brothers and she knew a relationship with that type of man would only cause problems.

I remember one time I was released from prison and she was pregnant with Candace and trust me when I say this: I cannot remember a time when she felt fear that I was aware of yet one night she called me crying and that's a no-no when it comes to her. She couldn't get it all out of her mouth that her boyfriend hit her before I found myself walking in a rage. She lived on Seventy-Second and I was on Twelfth Street. It didn't matter where I was I was coming to f-someone and something up. She needed me and I heard the fear in her voice and if I had never been there for her before this one time I was going to be there regardless the price.

At the time I was on parole till 2045 and if I got into any trouble it could cost me to have to spend the rest of my life behind bars. Didn't matter. I allowed prison and my selfish decisions to get in the way for years of my being there for my sister and this one time that she called on me I was getting to her even in a flood and I couldn't swim.

By the time a friend pulled up on me I was on Thirty-Eighth Street and he took me straight to her and I didn't ask questions when I pushed the door open. I just ran right up to him and gave him the butt kicking of his life and all I can remember is the rage I felt for this fool putting his hands on my sister and I wanted to make sure this was going to be a lesson to anybody don't put your hands on her period. All I knew was this will be something he is going to remember for the rest of his life.

My sister Samantha is and always will be my guardian angel and it doesn't matter what the issue is. I'll always sacrifice my life for her. It won't make up for the time missed but it will give me peace of mind and possibly her some reassurance that I got her back especially since so many of her tears went unanswered. It was like 13years of my life in prison and not to mention 12 parole violations and my addiction that got away from me that has no explanation of the truth to what my sister means to my life yet I always felt her prayers and her tears and I truly believe it was God's grace that kept it alive in my ears.

Damaged "But God"

Today my sister and her daughter Candace are just a few to mention that are apart of my biggest supporters in my quest to rebuild my life as a God-fearing man and although my journey has been up and down their prayers and many tears and examples of the way they live their lives gives me the courage to keep getting up when I fall for one of my sister's truest saying is, "I love you bro! you gotta know God has so much more for you." I know that today for all the many times God has shown his continuance grace and mercy in my life and I love you sis.

Damaged "But God"

When A Woman Cries

Watching an old movie that's full of romance,

Experiencing the expression on a woman's face

It is so sensual and enjoying that nothing could ever take its place

To be full of pain, nevertheless accepting her own tears

Exciting as it may be the birth of a child exposes her true fears

Some of us relating to the male satisfaction believe that dominating a woman's existence is a form of fame and even the ultimate high

Yet no one knows of the dreadful cry of a woman when she cries

She hopes for the world and God gives her a plan

Unexpectedly, she examines the illusion of a man

Still fighting the shame and guilt of false promises made from all the days before

She's left to ponder the process that led her godly soul beyond the heavens doors

There it is again her cry so full of pain

The beauty of sunshine that's turned into darkened rain

Trapped from hands too feet like an animal prisoner in chain

Always unfulfilling the emotions and fantasies of a woman as she's left with nothing to gain

The tears are never really apparent as one searches the eyes

Yet here I am today I tell you all it hurts!

When A Woman Cries

I love you, Mama and Sam

I Wonder

I wonder where would I be today

If my life and dreams went a different way

If I could overcome my addiction

And set new goals and stay firm within my convictions

I wonder if I could just change yesterday's thoughts

Would my tomorrow be paved in gold

With the lessons I've been taught?

I Wonder

I wonder if when the Lord made me did he have a true plan

Was I to be raised as an honest genuine man

Or is this the wrong time or just a mistake.

Either way, my life feels as though it's fake

I wonder if someone else is enjoying my role

And the nightmare I face

Has me buried deep in a hole.

I Wonder

I wonder if all I wonder is truly worth the while

As I sit here daily confused

I can't travel another mile.

Searching for answers, Lord knows I wonder

With the image of a vision I'm left to ponder

The identity of a secret that shall never require,

No past nor future of one's own desire

I Wonder

Damaged "But God"

Well about me—Chuck D!

I was protected since day one from everything except the drama and damaged caused by a life that was full of confusion and unacceptable views on how to relate to reality. From the time I can remember, I was always left alone mainly because of my lack of skills in sports. Although we were The Bowser Boys I never fit into the world my brothers enjoyed .While they participated in sports I was trying to figure out who and what would become of me.

I felt like I had nothing to offer in skills and with deep low self-esteem I figured my existence would be ignored. I used to try to walk and look like Carl and imagined myself to be as hard as Kenny. I learned at an early age that I could transform my reality into a fairy tale. I did such a good job at pretending that I made myself believe that my toy army men would play and fight for me when I had nowhere else to turn. The one thing that would surely keep me I hoped was my foundation in God, which Mom engraved in me. She would always say, "Keep your faith in the Lord. He won't leave you son." Even with all the support of my mother I never found that joy that would fill the void of not being able to measure up to Carl and Kenny.

As time would reveal I was easy to be influenced because I wanted to be accepted. I learned a lot from my brothers but the streets made me. I was on my porch watching and waiting for any opportunity to get my feet wet. I just wanted to be recognized and it didn't matter for what.

Lack of attention was and has always been my downfall, until one day this old-school hustler gave me one dollar to come shoot dice for him not knowing that I already knew how to play because Carl taught me. I did really good, so afterward he gave me $10 and at ten or eleven years old all I could think about was all the candy I could go buy and the attention it would bring my way. I remember that went on for weeks which became my after school project. I would even sneak out of church and out of the house late at night just to go play.

I never saw the addiction to it as an issue because the streets made it seem so fascinating with all the other enticements that came with getting money to play. Gambling led to stealing and then robbing whatever and whoever to stay in the game. No one showed the signs of failure because I assumed that nothing was wrong with being a beast in the hood not to mention that I was pretty good at gambling until it finally hit me by surprise one loss after another. And then desperation kicked in and that would cause me to adopt to a life of crime just to be a part of what I believed to be cool and fly.

Just remember, at age six, I told my mom I was going where my dad was because when I seen him in jail I felt so alone and I wanted him to be there for me yet never knowing that my behavior and all my bad choices would truly lead me right to him and ten years later that's what happened.

Damaged "But God"

My mother was forcing church and school down my throat every day trying to keep me from being apart of the statistics of the system and with all that she had seen with her own eyes with my father she overwhelmed herself in trying to get me into something different so she hoped.

I use to read my bible and prayed at first a lot until one day my cell was open up to go too church but when I enter the chapel it was full of predators and homosexuals and most of the inmates were (pc) protective custody. As I approached the door a guard pulled me to the side and asked me was I lost. I wasn't laughing then because of how naïve I was at 17 and in prison but I never went back to no church callout.

I met a lot of different people who made me become better in my criminal thinking and in getting adjusted to my new prison environment and all the rules. I watched guys get raped and die from suicide and or physically being attacked by more than one person. I had seen game being run on the best of them and I heard the cries of their screams daily. I even went through the trials of being tested and I knew one thing about me in that world period: I was not gay and most definitely wasn't going to be gay and no one was going to push me in a corner no matter what. Once I put that mask on I became immune to the bullshit not to mention when I found out that I could really fight I pushed myself to a place where nothing mattered because it was never about the fight but about the win. I didn't care about being pretty I only wanted to win cause a fight goes on and on but a win is final and I began to set the stage for my reality while behind those walls. Still a lot of the inmates just didn't get it and got caught up in homosexual activities and all the foolish games. I didn't understand their theory of prey or predator but I watched as they got lost in their reality of life behind those walls.

Prison was crazy and people don't understand it but it's so fast in there especially in the 1980s, yet it had its flaws and one of my missions was to find out what they were if it didn't involve me being forced into not being a man and or abused then it was my motivation to put me in control of some type of power over what I was seeing.

I learned that people would listen to me because I was good with putting a lot words together even if it didn't make sense and what was funny is I just needed one person to consider rather or not if it sounded good for the rest of them to respond and follow my lead and before long I had all the attention. That was really as I called it then a great investment and quality to have cause it gave me the opportunity to stand out and everyone believed that I could almost change the course of their false sense of reality.

And that caught the attention of the women guards and nurses that later prove to be an asset in the time of need. I had my share of depression and anxiety that prison put you through while learning to function in the system. The one thing I never forgot was that this is not my home and whatever manipulation I had forced on someone I used it to the fullest because I didn't want to lose my hope that one day I would be free and not mention before they used it on me.

I can remember one time I called my mother at the very beginning of my incarceration crying because I wanted to go home and didn't believe I could handle all the drama and madness in prison. The fear of everything around me just made me feel trapped and the one person I believed could rescue me was my mom and for the first time in my life the realization hit me there was nothing she could do for me. I heard it in her voice right before she hung up on me with tears coming down her face. She said, "I love you, Charles, but you got to stop this crying and deal with this situation cause you did this and Mama can't help you." And the phone went dead.

From that day forward I closed my mind off to all and any emotions to the outside world because I was now doomed and had to become a beast and or monster that needed to survive so I thought.

Damaged "But God"

Throughout all the fear and recklessness I had endured on my first bid down I had to try to come too some type of peace with God because in there you got to believe in something especially with all the many clicks that surrounded you like Moes, Beys , Aryan Brotherhood, Crips and Bloods and GDs and the few Christian. There was something for everyone to be apart of and most of it was a trap because guys were joining groups for protection and or forced too.

My mom kept her persistence in making sure she announced God's presence in my life even though it wasn't evidence that I had the spirit in me as I walked around the prison but I did and as the days became years it was over before I even knew it. My mother did make it easy also because she kept money on my books and I can remember getting money every month. She would send me 5 to 25 dollars every week and back then that was a lot. Remember that this was the '80s and having money truly made it easy not to get trapped by the predators and the prison gangs.

As I said from the beginning my Mom was indeed a God fearing woman and because of her constant prayers God kept me safe regardless of all the mischief I was involved in while doing my time he allowed me to make my first parole board hearing. I know it was the Lord cause even though I didn't let the time break me it was truly his grace that held me down in all of my foolishness. Cause I did everything I could to buck the system every chance I had. In my mind that negative attention made me a monster and I enjoyed it. And I guess even though this was a totally different atmosphere I still wanted everyone to know that I was a Bowser and like Carl and Kenny growing up everybody knew the Bowser Boys. I was going to make sure it was known in the penitentiary as well.

Damaged "But God"

I was released on August 17, 1989 and although I didn't do a lot of praying I could feel the prayers of my mom as she prayed constantly for my safety and freedom. I walked out the first time in a while a free man yet controlled by my demons of institutionalized thinking and mental health depression.

And just knowing I didn't deal with issues that would create a better me while in prison. I got my GED and a barber's license. None of it was for a new beginning but for the purpose so I could move around in the prison without being noticed. I achieved those certificates so I could be able to have movement to participate in any and all illegal activities I was involved in. So when I came home I wasn't prepared for anything but my return to prison whenever that time came because the one thing I knew for sure was that I was coming back.

I never did drugs to the extreme till I went to prison mainly just to cope because you had to be high in order to withstand the trauma and the mental games of daily living. So when I came home I was sneaking off using heroin in the closet and smoking weed daily and experimenting with cocaine and crack. My way of holding on to the wall as everything was dropping in front on me was to just stay high as I did in prison and I seriously I forgot to take off my mask and didn't give myself a thought of a chance to succeed. I felt as though I missed out on so much and everybody owed me something and those that didn't became easy prey to my criminal behavior. Right off the top I was doomed for failure and just didn't care. But the fact is I didn't know how to live free for real because when I say I wasn't broken I was actually broken mentally.

Damaged "But God"

In November of 1989, I had only been home for less than three months. I was in the streets trying to get that attention once again that Carl was getting in the dope game. We were both older and free and I just wanted to make one power move that would put me and Carl back on top. I just watched Carl lose over 5,000 dollars in two days gambling. We sold the drugs we had fast to try to get back in the game and we lost that as well. With the fronts gone and no way out. I convinced a friend to help us. He made something happen for me and I asked Carl to go with me to deliver it to someone I thought was cool. Carl didn't want to and even overslept the next day which was the first sign. Yet we went to the meeting place anyway at the old Indian Springs shopping center. It was like something out of the movies. Hundreds of ATF agents and other federal agents on point. We had been set up by a close childhood friend. Damn, all I could think about was that Carl kept saying he didn't feel right and he really didn't want to go now look at what I did to us both. While being held Carl screamed through the vents for me to be quiet. I didn't realize until my cell down open that something was wrong because I didn't see Carl until I was freed and I had seen the back of Carl in the courtroom and my mother shouted out with tears flowing down her face, "It should have been you Charles. You have never been nothing and once again you got Carl in trouble."

I understood then that Carl took the rap for us both by saying the drugs was his. All my life Carl stood up for his younger brothers. Seeing that and feeling my mother's pain left me numb and more damaged in my quest to find my true worth. I went back to robbing and doing more drugs because of the guilt. My addiction consumed me and my world just dropped without a doubt. I lost all hope and just couldn't get right.

This was the first time I felt the damage I imposed on someone else. That someone was Carl.

I went back to prison on parole violation after violation—in fact two times in one year. Then one day after staying high for several days I went on a robbery spree and committed so many crimes that I seriously don't even remember half of them. They caught up to me on October 21, 1990. I was arrested and convicted to 35years to life in prison. Once again my life became doomed. Damaged "But God"

In 1991, I married Tray my childhood girlfriend while in the county in hope to gain some form of stability and I guess I needed to know that I was still alive. Tray was my first love and at the time I didn't realize how my actions and selfishness could and would damage her life.

Tray was the second young woman's life I ruined my mother's was the first. I just didn't want to do my time alone yet although I really loved her, she was young and had her whole life ahead of her. I remember when I was sentenced. I turned away from the judge in hope that my mother and Tray didn't see my reaction of disbelief as I felt my legs buckled yet I knew I had to stand firm or at least attempt to because hearings the judge say as loud as clear 35 to life aww hell I surely didn't want them to see that fear of no return but as only as I knew how to do I put that mask on immediately as I faced my family and smiled only to see and hear my mom cry out to the Lord God for strength. Those heartbroken tears again, I knew I was truly killing her from the inside out.

Damaged "But God"

When I return to my cell I cried so hard because I ruined Carl's life and my own. After a few days of sleep I began praying asking God for direction but he never answered so I made up my mind that I would wake up every day to die so just in case one of these fools killed me in here it would be expected and seriously what purpose did I have to live.

I left Tray out there by herself to take care of our first daughter Hope alone and I found out before I left for prison she was having our second daughter Faith and now everything was hitting me all at once the reality that my girls were going to be without their dad just as me and my brothers were without ours that cycle of the curse that was Charles Bowser one and two just don't fit in this world especially as fathers.

So as time went on I finally was sent back to the walls and for the first time in many years I was reunited with my father and trust me it wasn't at all what I hoped for. They called him Big Chuck and I can remember coming to the Lansing Correctional Facility and this man was standing along the wall with a crew of other inmates and a few of them were homosexuals. My dad had a red bandanna around his head and really stood out. I off the top knew he was important. As I walked down the sidewalk the guard told me I was going to A- cell house and at the time it was called animal house. And it was such a sight to see because everyone was moving around as if they were on the streets and I mean this place was wide open.

I remember like it was just yesterday. I moved to cell 305 and already there was a guy living in there who pissed me off on the first day and I beat him down and put him out of the cell and later that evening one of my dad's friends came down and put a care package on my bed. I refused it because at the time I haven't seen my dad in almost fourteen years or whatever so I wasn't accepting anything even though this guy looked like me and I pointed him out at first sight. I still didn't know if I could trust him cause this is prison and I've seen my shares of tricks. Plus I heard it to many times from the Bandits yea young blood I know your family hell I'm almost like a uncle to you take this package and whenever you need anything just let me know and then comes the trap one night you in your cell and that so call uncle gets horny and he is reminded of all the favors he done for you and it's pay up time wow seriously that's how it goes and I have seen it time and time again get done to the best. But never me I didn't except nothing and I mean nothing unless "I TOOK IT" from you and you know what that meant.

Later he came to my cell and we talked and talked and as I watched him talk and just his demeanor and everything about him was a reflection of me and I knew he was for sure my Dad and the good was still in him and I remember he said to me, "You may not agree with what you hear and/or see while you are here but I am your father. But my world isn't like yours and this is my life. I love you but do your time and don't judge me and from here on I'm Big Chuck and nothing else.

Now I understood everything he was saying yet even though I did my first time in Hutchinson Correction and knew how to do time it was indeed a different ball game in Lansing. It was like a history lesson with no emotions or feelings, yet I understood and what's funny is that one day I was down by his cell and he had this photo album that was full of articles and pictures of Carl and Kenny sports activities and pictures of his family, us—my mother and his boys, the Bowser Boys and what excited me even more was that he had a Bible that had a marker that was on Psalm 23, and seeing that took me way back to when my mother would make us remember Psalm 23:

> The Lord is my shepherd; I shall not want. He maketh me lie down in green pastures; he leadth me beside the still waters. He restoreth my soul; he leadth me in the paths of righteousness for his name's sake. Yea though I walk through the valley of the shadow of death, I will fear no evil; for thou art with me. Thy rod and staff they comfort me. Thou prepared a table before me in the presence of my enemies; thou anointed my head with oil; my cup runneth over. Surely, goodness and mercy shall follow me all the days of my life; and I will dwell in the house of the Lord forever and forever and ever. Amen.

Over the years this scripture was important to my survival while I was in prison. Facing a 35 to life was hard enough that I needed the word of God and just to know I had hope which that scripture brought it gave me a sense of peace. It also meant I was done with life as a free man physically but spiritually I could still depend on the Lord. And what I didn't know at the time was that God was already working his hands in my situation and he was just waiting on me to see his plans for me were so much bigger than I could imagine he needed my attention and what better place to get it in.

Damaged "But God"

Like I said it was different in Lansing because it was more about fighting in Hutchinson and in Lansing it was about killing and don't get me wrong you can get killed anywhere doing time it just takes the right motivation and the determination to prove a point and it's like that life over it's just that simple being locked up with animals and monsters with no regards to human life cause they don't care about themselves plus who cares what happens in the jungle all the guards main concern is that they make it out alive and there were times they didn't.

I had to really readjust my position in my thinking when I got to Lansing because once again it was no room for mistakes and being that it was so open you could get lost without no one knowing. And that's what was great about being locked up with Big Chuck he watched my every move from a distance and even when I didn't know he was watching he was and I was doing some pretty crazy things like robbing the drug pushers in prison and gambling as if I never left the streets. I remember getting into with this big muscle bound Muslim in the gym because he took our stash and dude was strong one of the stronger cats in prison. As I approached him he started saying jokes about my eye like you one eye bi— what you gonna do and I just said meet me in the bathroom and he came but continued to talk and before he knew it I was walking back to the unit with my stash in hand and he was knocked out laying on the floor still in the bathroom. By the time I got to the unit my Dad Big Chuck was on the upper deck waiting on me with a sword sharp and ready telling me to get behind him cause he knew it wasn't going to end there. But even after they came in a pack the guy I knocked out he didn't want anymore of me but either way Big Chuck let it be known if you don't want to die today gon back to your dorms cause nobody is touching my son. My Dad!!!

Before getting to a point where I understood that I was getting nowhere in prison I went through a lot of pain and suffering just trying to fit in and it came a time that I figured I needed to focus on trying to give some of my time back. And let me say I had no knowledge that anything was wrong with my case cause I most definitely did whatever they said I did well like I said earlier I was so high I didn't remember much but if they said I did it then it's very possible I did.

Damaged "But God"

Out of no way God made away it's called judge and jury ExParte Communication which is illegal term for a judge to have a discussion with any jury without the present of myself and my attorney in regards to the consideration of a verdict in my trial. After reading in my transcripts that one of the jurors wanted to be excused and the judge forced her to stay it was then considered a mistrial and by law we should have been made known of it but wasn't. I put in those hours at the Law Library and God open my eyes so I could see a flaw and Hallelujah Thank you God. My case was overturned and my sentence was vacated and I was headed back to the county.

On March 6th 1993 actually on my mother's birthday I got the news to pack up my belongings I was being transferred out and it's amazing how quickly we forget about God and all his wonders. I wasn't there a week waiting to see if they were going to retry me when I broke another inmates jaw and was locked down facing assault charges omg what is this about once again I allowed me to get in the way of God's blessing. Sitting on lockdown the D.A made a special visit to come see me and threatened me with both being tried all over and a new case of assault if I didn't plead out to just 2 robbery charges ran with my old 5 to 20 which would give me a 15 to 60 and after processing it all and what could happened in the result of a new trial I took the deal hell I don't have the 35 to life and in my mind I believed I would be seeing the Parole Board immediately and would be going home wow my best thinking has always been my worst thinking.

In my life there has been a lot of damage that has caused the reaction to my mental and spiritual healing and in one way or another I've allowed it to engulfed my institutionalized thinking and behavior to a point where it made me unable to face reality and believe that it is a form of normality to drown yourself in regrets and fear in order to be safe with no true expectations.

With the excitement of being given another chance at freedom no longer with the 35 to life. I could breathe and try to prepare myself to be human at least in the very near future. Unknown to me there was a greater storm coming that would shatter my heart and world and surely destroy my hope for life.

I got into a fight with this guy from the city a week earlier and after our struggle he shouted out to me I'm going to do you like they did your brother! At the time it didn't hit me because I knew nothing was going on with any of my brothers. But on a Tuesday afternoon I was called for a visit but what was strange was there were no visits on Tuesday, especially not at the Medium in Lansing.

I entered the visiting room and was met by the chaplain. I couldn't put it together and he wouldn't address me but said, "I'm waiting on your family." I stared at the metal door. It seemed like hours until it finally opened.

My mother came in followed by my wife at the time Tray, and my brother Kenny. I was confused. I didn't understand what was going on. I thought maybe something was going on with my sister Samantha because she wasn't there. The chaplain asked me to take a seat and I was like, "What's going on? Why are you guys here? Where is my sister is she okay?"

All of a sudden the room became dark and I heard the words "They killed Carl." It was like my soul was evaporating before my eyes like I couldn't breathe and my insides all my organs just stopped. I blacked out only to be awakened with the same reality. Oh God, oh God, how? Why? This can't be true. Carl is locked up. He wouldn't let that happen to himself.

Damaged "But God"

November 1993, a month after his 30th birthday Carl's life was taken over a basketball game in his pride played in important role. All I could think of was *It should have been me. Why God?*

I was able to go to Carl's funeral but in full shackles. As I walked into the place, I saw family and friends that really did not matter to me. I just wanted to hold my brother. With every fear every tear every thought and all the emotions that I covered up for so many years came rushing out. I hadn't cried in a long while and just for a second that mask that was a part of my existence finally disappeared.

I tried to get in that casket because I knew Carl needed me and I hoped I wasn't too late. He was just sleeping. *Get up Carl I can't do this life alone. Please let me help you breathe. Get up, wake up!* to this date I have not attended another funeral. Closure is final.

I will never say goodbye to you Carl.

Damaged "But God"

Trying to find myself after leaving the funeral I had to make myself put the mask back on that kept me safe for so long—only this time the mask was softened with a different view because I realized that dying in prison wasn't going to be my legacy to the end of my story although throughout my entire prison stay I became institutionalized and at one point I just didn't know if I could make it on the outside because I had become so comfortable with the setting of being caged. I became trapped in the prison I created around the prison I was physically in that whenever I was faced with anything that required me to feel and or show emotions I would revert to my mental health diagnosis and play crazy yet the truth was I had lost my mind and my reasoning to live so I wasn't playing I was crazy.

I remember a guard approached me once and said, "Do you not know you are a leader and people listen to you? Why don't you fight the good fight of encouragement and use your ability for a different purpose? At that time I didn't understand what that was but I knew that wasn't the first time I heard that. It was as though after Carl's death the foolishness didn't matter anymore and although I was trying to make sense of it all I seriously still wanted to hurt someone something anything but yet I was totally struggling trying to carry out that mission because my thoughts were not matching up to my feelings.

Trying my best to ignore the advice of both God and my surroundings I needed to move on but I had to once again find a mask that would help me isolate and become that monster that didn't care and hopefully would show self-destruct and the beginning of my quest for suicidal thoughts.

Damaged "But God"

After many ups and downs with my fighting off the thoughts to kill myself I had to settle down and prepare myself for the Parole Board and I couldn't understand why it was so hard to persuade the Kansas Parole Board to let me go home. Then it came to me one night sitting on the edge of my bed. All those attributes that I had were fine and cool that I learned while in prison manipulation and power to control were all good in there but it wasn't the God in me. I Believed I had what it took to get over on anyone for if they just listened to me for five minutes I could hook and sink them but that was my institutionalized thinking and for many years it fooled even me but it didn't do anything for the Parole Board.

Damaged while in prison I experimented with many type of drugs from marijuana and cocaine to my drug of choice: heroin.

One thing for sure drugs on the inside was more abundant than on the outside and out of all the years I've done it's crazy but I knew of only four to five overdoses unlike in the free world. For sure the tolerance level couldn't go high because of the security level of access to move around was indeed almost impossible. Yet the drugs at that time wasn't considered as an addiction but a means to cloud the body from association or detachment from reality of the walls that held us (me) from what I would possibly never be able to love which was life.

There was a time when I received a dirty UA every month for eight months straight in and out of the hole and restriction 30 days at a time. It had gone on for so long that when it was time for me to see the parole board I would get denied year after year and although it hurt and killed me on the inside yet on the outside as long as I was high and had the attention of a few female guards I was content with the outcome.

Until one day my childhood love Tray came to see me and she was crying when I walked out into the visiting room and I asked her why the tears and she said, "I miss you." I don't know what or why but hearing that knocked me back a step and something came over me. I just knew that there was so much more beyond those walls that had kept me trapped in confusion for so many years and when I was walking back I began to cry out, "God send your spirit. Lead and show me how to go home." And once again not my timing but Gods, he did the impossible.

Damaged "But God"

Chapter 3
Freedom

Damaged "But God"

The year 1996 was unlike any year I've ever encountered, all the emotions that I held end in order to survive while behind the walls I had to learn to replace with something that would at least give me a chance. I had to fight off my own false reality from deep in the shadows of the valley of my mind for it was full of corruption and death. Seeing that shift of what was to come I had to come to terms with life and death mainly because of the mask that was formed to give me justification of why I didn't exist. It had to be released so I could become free in the mind. I was released from prison with a hundred dollars in my pocket to take on a different demon that was far greater than any demon those prison walls could have unleashed upon me

Damaged "But God"

Understanding a new way of thinking was a must and not knowing what life was about I had to restructure my ability to be adaptable to freedom. My family was still in turmoil over the death of Carl and went about it in silence as if he didn't exist and although it was tough at first I had to pull my head out of the clouds.

Once released things began to change when me and my first wife Tray got back together. As soon as we did she got pregnant with our third child Charles Jr which brought joy to my soul. We already had Hope and

Faith who were the most beautiful girls I had ever seen. It was a struggle for Tray and myself mainly because of my being institutionalized and all the behaviors I brought home that had me trapped.

Over the years I also realized that I had severe mental health issues because of all I had been through. I was unable to replace that mask which was the blanket to my peace that caused so many problems in our marriage. For one I didn't know how to raise a child because in my own reality I was still a child in my mind and I just felt that I missed out on so much and with that said I couldn't be the man I've always hoped to be to Tray. I could not be true to myself nor to anyone for that matter cause I really didn't know who I was and seriously in my mind I kept wondering how I could ever match up to the life Tray had already experienced without me. So many years had gone and came and I was so confused and lost with no real sense of identity.

Coming home to Tray truly broken didn't help our relationship. Going to prison at a young age and leaving the love of my life while she was 15 was damaging within itself and we tried to recreate our past only to see we had both grown so far apart.

Tray was really the first girl I ever cared about. I remember I used to see her at school everyday after I first noticed her in the Gateway projects. As beautiful as ever and let me say off the top she never noticed me and seriously I don't believe she even looked my way once. I remember she was walking through the hood and I was gambling in the park. When I saw her I immediately stopped shooting during my shot and I ran to her and because I was winning I showed my handful of money. At the age sixteen I was already known in the hood as a gambler because that was my hustle. As I approached her I asked her, "What's your name?" She responded, "Tray!" It still sends chills down my neck because at fourteen she was breathtaking and even then all the guys were on her and her sister Mimi. Beautiful!

She gave me her name but that was it. I found out where she stayed and no I'm not a stalker but I would be waiting for her bus everyday after school because at that time I was suspended from school so I made it a point that I wouldn't stop showing up until she was apart of my life. One day as I was waiting for her bus me and my friends broke into someone's house. Thinking that everything was good afterward I met up with Tray at the bus stop and as I walked her home only to be approached by a moving car and guys jumping out and chasing me and shooting. I can only imagine what she thought witnessing this scary moment but I turned to her and said "I'll be back" and then took off.

I never understood the dysfunction of my actions and what was yet to come. I came back later to Tray's house and sat on her porch for hours and told her I wasn't going to leave until she said she would be my girlfriend. She still says years later that she said it only to get me to leave her porch but I know for real that she couldn't resist my nice looks and bad-boy behavior.

Our relationship was short-lived because all my destructive decisions caught up to me and I went to prison in 1984 for robbery. Who knows what our life would have been like had I had the chance to become something different. Yet her life and mine were doomed.

Damaged "But God"

My first year at home in the free world was full of recklessness and drugs. I didn't take the time to raise my children but I raised my addictions to drugs and criminal behavior to a full-time high. My favorite pastime adventures were gambling and getting high. As thousands ran through my hands the hype began to trap me so deep in the foolishness that I completely lost the comfort of my home and children and Tray.

The responsibility of raising three kids and be a husband was not what I expected. At the time I found it more exciting chasing the dice game than I did being a husband and or father. After being locked down for so long I didn't know how be comfortable in a relationship. I remember after a few good loses in gambling and not being accountable as a father I became depressed. I know many times Tray wanted to move on because I just wasn't living up to what she expected and even still she took a chance on me because we had our kids and she wanted to at least try to help us be a family and although I wasn't giving God any attention she was and one morning she asked me to go to church with her and the kids. It was such a great moment because I didn't know it but Tray was asking the church to pray for me already so when I went to church the entire church knew who I was and for the first time in a while I felt the spirit of the Lord just moving me and I hoped that it would bring about a change in my life. After going to church a few weeks I slowly began to feel alive and I started trying to figure out how I could find my way back to the Lord so I could get my family back but there were some things I needed to get in order first like my drug addiction and the gambling it all was apart of my selfish ways and the destructive patterns that kept me trapped. I had to get on track with what Tray was searching for cause it was apparent that she knew what she wanted and that was me. We started making it right and I a job and things were going good for awhile I even stopped using but couldn't stop gambling and it wasn't long before I went back to my old ways. I had responsibilities and my kids needed me yet I wanted the easy way out and hustling wasn't helping but only sending me down a dark road all over again.

The thing I didn't realize was with me or without Tray was committed to our children and didn't hesitate at the first sign of trouble to go on living without to keep our children safe and just like my mother she willing to do it alone because I made it clear that I couldn't separate my way of living.

At the end of 1996, I was in the streets hustling and trying to run from my obligation of being a man and father again. While at a friend's barbershop I started a conversation with a young lady that was cute and down to earth and from our conversation she didn't have kids and she just wanted to chill. Vee was special yet my intentions were not. We had a relationship while I was still married and my fourth child was born. Erin was so little and beautiful, but she suffered from complications at birth. I must admit that at first I was so confused because I knew the commitment expected of me by Vee wasn't going to be fulfilled because I was still married to Tray and I still wasn't ready to let go. Although I did love Vee and was so excited for the birth of our daughter I just couldn't get my mind off of my situation with Tray. Having our three children and deceived in my bullshit wasn't fair and I knew I had to make a decision or do what I've always done when it came to dealing with emotions. I got high and put all four of my children and both Tray and Vee out of my mind. Again I was in my prison and with each hit I watched the tears roll down my face cause there it was again doomed I ruined and damaged the lives of others.

In 1997, I went back to prison for a parole violation. I was released again at the end of 1997 and came home to four children: Hope, Faith, Charles Jr and Erin. I never made it right with Vee because I really changed her entire life. I never meant to cause her any pain but I did and she truly did deserve so much better than what I had to offer her and Erin.

Erin grew up alone all her life with a man she called Dad regardless of what she was told about him (me).The world I envisioned while in prison was totally misleading. I believed that I would come home and enjoy life in away that the glamour of the streets would make me happy and most definitely rich. I visioned fast women and cars and quick money. Yet not understanding my own issues with abandonment and trust and mental health issues I set out to destroy and damage everything that crossed my path.

Out of all my children the one who suffered the most like me from the beginning was Erin—abandoned and not valued and once again the story of my life. The greatest thing Erin had in life was there no constant reminder of failure and let downs that I brought time and time again like I did into my other kids life.

Damaged "But God"

After going back to prison two more times and failing in my marriage and as a father to all four of my kids I was left trying to put the pieces back together and I just got to say as long as I was willing to run from my fears nothing was ever going to change for me. While back in prison I started seeing a mental health counselor so I could work through some of my issues and once again I realize I had a deep fear of dying and being alone yet all my life that's all I did was run everyone away and put a lot of energy in trying to kill myself and the only way to deal with any of it was to stay high and for once I needed something more. First, I had to deal with one major problem, my mental health issues. Depression, PTSD, bipolar disorder, and suicidal thoughts. I needed help and I asked for it because I realized that something had to change.

I remember my very first time being incarcerated. I felt so alone trapped in a hole with vultures trying to steal everything. I can remember being so scared I once called my mom crying so hard and believing and wishing I was dead because the pressure was killing me. I promised to be good I told her. Only to see then I could never be good after that experience because all my cries for help left me traumatized beyond repair. Being on my fourth parole violation and lost in my fears mixed with my prison mentality, I told myself I had to open myself up to something new whatever that may be and I knew I had find that peace with God so I spent most of my time praying and studying and learning the Serenity Prayer in hopes for a change with the help of the program.

Once released from prison a fourth time in 1998, I had a new outlook on life. Knowing and believing I could do my part to stay alive and free. I got a job working at a car lot and when I went in for the interview hoping to get the job for detailing cars the owner heard my voice and came out and took over the interview; and the next morning I came to work as an intern car salesman and as a collections manager. Once again my conversation one of my most important skills of survival got me a job.

Damaged "But God"

While working that job I provided for my children and got back into my gambling habit and although I did everything I could while back in prison to change my patterns of destruction it was once again my way and God was put on the back burner. One evening I was off work at a car wash and noticed this angel wiping down her car. I approached her and said, "I know I may be the ugliest guy you'll ever meet yet if you ever feel ugly please give me a call and I promise I'll make you beautiful. All the while there were other guys trying to talk to her and get her attention and she wasn't having it but I did notice she was very focused on me and let me say when I approached her I was very confident that I wouldn't receive the same reaction she gave them so before I left I gave her a business card from my job and asked her to call me.

Shy was so beautiful and unlike any woman that I've ever met and for real to contradict myself from my statement earlier of being confident that was just because of the competition that was at the car wash lol but seriously I didn't think after I left that I had any chance with her but out of the blue she called. We talked on the phone and I invited her out. I never had so much fun in my life we went to the casino and afterwards to the club and as we walked into the club she was so surprised cause it was like I was a celebrity we were served and watched as if it was a red carpet event.

Shy didn't know about my being incarcerated or about my criminal past and I wanted to keep it that way. She had a way about herself that all my friends and family and even strangers would stop and stir at her and her beauty was such an amazing sight to see. Shy had all the qualities of a boss she had a great job and very ambitious to be at the top of her career and her work ethic's was just remarkable. And it was always a great revelation to know that she worked for Hallmarks Card cause my mother worked there in the early years when it was Hall's.

She had that it factor and I was lost in lust of it all.

As I look back at our relationship I don't think neither of us expected it to last as long as it did. It was supposed to be fun just to hang out and be seen with one another but I got to admit it wasn't long before I knew I wanted more and it was like I just kept showing up and we really did do something everyday as if it was the first time.

What I knew about Shy, she was very particular about life and what she wanted to accomplish and driven by goals and it's so funny cause I was opposite but curious as to what it would look like to be successful so she brought stability to my life and I brought excitement to her life like just getting up going places without planning was not her but that was my idea of excitement. At first we complemented each other and areas that were unfamiliar and it felt right.

We were having so much fun and it never really did come up much or did many questions about my past until one day I had to explain why I was on Parole and I'm not sure if I really surprised her cause I believe she was ok with the honesty and the fact that I was doing my part and making life changing decisions. From the beginning I always made sure Shy was safe and out of my private life and although I was doing a lot of gambling I was actually winning and I kept up my fronts.

When I met her family for the first time her mom called me a smooth talker lol. And what was so apparent in their family dynamics was that they were very proud and close. Each one of her sisters were direct and to the point about Shy's future for all three of them were very educated and rising in their careers. Whenever I was around them I have to be totally honest I was embarrassed because I just didn't fit in although they did everything they could to make me comfortable. I just never seen a family so structured with values and the will to be great and when I met her dad I was so intimidated by him cause you talk about a man that had everything together he did and he was the motivation to their family and didn't except excuses not at all.

I remember we went to New York because her younger sister was getting married and I remember that I would just tag alone behind everyone and her mother slowed down and began to walk at my paste just to make sure I didn't feel left out and I'm telling you at that moment I knew I was apart of that family. I can also remember the food they prepared I was not familiar with and one day I was asked to try a dish and refused and her mom was very vocal about it even though she was short in height she can bring you down to her size fast lol I was told how can you be a guest in someone home and not be willing to try new things you don't know what you like if you have never tried it and after that embarrassing moment I never refused anything she made lol and to be honest I loved everything she cooked especially Ghormeh Sabzi and Scorched Rice and if you didn't know it Shy was Iranian.

I learned all that I knew from the streets and I didn't know what it was like to be in a functional family setting but seeing their connection as a whole made me realize what all I truly missing growing up. I learned more from Shy and her family than I ever learned from anyone. But because of my institutionalize thinking and my criminal behavior I just couldn't find away to reach a point of understanding where what they were showing me that I deserved it.

While in New York surprisingly to us both Shy became pregnant and 7 months later our son Amir was born almost 3 months early and had a lot of complications and because Shy had Preeclampsia during her delivery of our son it was a chance that she may not have made it so a C-section was done to save them both. At that time like always I hadn't acknowledged God in a long while but when I was called to the hospital and they told me Shy asked for me and she said Charles please save our son in all my life it amaze me how a mother will sacrifice it all for her child and it blows my mind cause that's what God did for us he gave his only son to die for our sins wow.

Shy came through and so did Amir bless his little soul he had so many tubes in his body and so tiny but was a fighter just like his mom and I remember when we brought him home for the first time we were all fighting over Shy and she went off on us saying please I just had a baby can you all just stop and give me a break it was so funny because I think we were fussing over some frozen lasagna about how to cook it lol. Shy was indeed a trooper and it wasn't many times that I can remember when she got upset but when she did wow it wasn't nice.

Before our son Amir was born, Shy and I got married and although we had some challenging times we did love each other and at the beginning it wasn't apparent all the demons I had hidden. We went through so much because I couldn't, nor did I know how to fit in her world and with my addictions to the streets she refused to completely ignore my habits because she understood that the effects could and would affect her own life.

The expectations in our relationship was crazy cause Shy was grounded and she knew how to separate the fantasy I was projecting from what was reality. She could be able to compartmentalize situations and address it all in a manner where she could still sleep at night but me on the other hand just couldn't get pass the hopes without works version in the way of life basically saying I wanted the world but didn't want to work for it and when I didn't see the outcome I wanted it would destroy me cause I then would make a mountain out of nothing pushing me over the edge. Shy didn't believe in excuses and she made none especially when it came to my addictions. She believed that there is a answer to anything and always focused on the solution not the problem and because of that her process in dealing with life is head on and her fight for the many issues we were having was always the same I was the problem.

Shy gave me the opportunity to become great and move forward from my criminal past and it was going so good that it scared me. Experiencing all the new ways of living life and the support from her family that were genuine and true for even they wanted the best for me and I began to believe that there was a chance that I could possibly be a positive factor in society.

It should have made me press forward but the pressure of the expectations and accountability overwhelmed me cause in my delusional mind and thoughts I made myself believe that I don't deserve to be happy and what the hell it won't last before everyone sees that I'm a failure and all my demons will show my true worth. Shy and Amir were surely worth more than I could give of myself. And what time would reveal is that it wasn't rather I was worthy of Shy and her family's love the truth to the matter was I was afraid of success and I didn't know what it would be like so I was not willing to just let myself feel the shift in my life I was use to less and it showed.

I spent those early years with Amir and I watch him say his first words and shoot his first basketball and even write his name just a few of the many things I had the pleasure of doing with him that I hope he never forgets. I missed out on all those things with my other kids. I never got to see Hope and Faith say their first words and I never took Erin to a doctor's appointment and I didn't have the chance to talk to Charles Jr about peer pressure. In each one of my children I left the lasting impression of how to run out on their family cause that's what I did over and over again.

Everyday of my life I will forever wonder "what if" when it comes to my kids and only God knows my heart because I only wanted what was best for all of them and the older I get I see truly how impaired my thoughts were cause as a kid all I wanted was for my dad just to show up just once and I know that's all Hope, Faith, Erin and Charles Jr and Amir ever wanted as well.

Damaged "But God"

Shy made it a point to keep me involved in Amir's daily function and most of times I wanted it just as much to be everything Amir could ever need and want. While my hopes was high in being a father Shy also pushed me to be even better at reaching out to all my other children. I will forever be grateful to Shy cause she did anything and all she could for each one of my children although they weren't her responsibility she treated them as if they were and made them apart of her life.

Throughout our thirteen years of marriage and relationship I realize that in my life there is a season and a reason for everything and Shy played an important role in my seasons for many reasons. I brought excitement into her life and she brought structure in mine. Shy was so different and I watched a strong woman get stronger no matter how damaged my own world had gotten because of my decisions.

On April 8, 2001, my life almost came to a deadly halt. I was stabbed ten times by four guys and was critically injured but I still had the strength to walk away only to wake up from a coma. And I cried my eyes out because I finally had a chance to die and couldn't even do that right. Oh, how I wished I was dead. Why God? Why are you saving me when I deserve death?

Damaged "But God"

I believe that after coming home from the hospital God had his reasons and I fought off the desires of my addiction and took the time to write up a program called Youth Awareness Life with A Vision and RACE (Recognizing Achievable Conscious Emotions). The program would embrace the truth for hope in our youth and hopefully change their core beliefs that lead them to destructive behaviors and habits and I could totally relate because of what road my life had taken. It would also build structure and awareness of a new sense of freedom that would give them a purpose to belong too something more in life.

RACE was so important because for me being trapped in the system for so many years and not knowing how to feel nor did I recognize what it meant to feel because of all the damage and setbacks that I was dealing with like guilt and grief and all the mental health issues. I wanted to create a program that would acknowledge the fear of acceptance and hope that it would encourage someone to see beyond what they learned from the streets and in the system and in broken homes and in life. Helping one to see past the pain and hurt by understanding where they are now is the start cause I never seen the beginning I only experienced the ending of my issues cause it was easier to except mines as damaged.

At first it was hard because everyone I tried to get help from shut me down because of my prison record and my many relapses on parole. No one understood that my experience alone was enough to motivate me to show results. Once Shy and I ran it across my parole officer she took a chance on it and me. We started the program at the parole office. At first it was going well until it was shut down due to DOC protocol that no one on parole could be in control of a program without supervision. Jenny my parole officer at the time did all she could to aid the program but was overloaded with her own cases so it was shut down.

At that time Shy and I were building on our relationship and trying to raise Amir. After getting the program shut down Jenny continue to help me because she seen that I was focus and she didn't want me to give up so she introduced me to a number of important people who could help me deliver my message in a different direction —not to mention the prison was reaching out to me to help with a Father's Day video that I did because at that time still my own father was still in prison. Also because of my many years of being in the system I kept a good relationship with many of the staff because while in prison I use to cut a lot of their hair and in doing so I use tell them what I hoped to do one day and there came a time when they wanted me to speak to a panel of parole board members, correctional officers, probation officers, and State Office members on what was working for me while I was on parole and what I was doing to maintain my life as a free man.

My life was moving so fast it was as though I had a new chance at life and being a father and husband. Shy and Amir brought that fire and energy that I had longed for and she believed in me. Fighting to change and finish the race of this unknown freedom was exciting and once again I could feel a sense of success. I went all over Lawrence and Topeka and Kansas City telling my story about what I was doing but not how God gave me another chance at life and brought my attention back to accomplishing something in life. This is my pattern in most of my life I get consumed by the attention and I fail to see how God's mercy and grace is behind it all and its never long after do I fall on my face.

The Bible says stand guard of your faith because Satan is out to kill and destroy you at all times especially in a moment of weakness. I began to allow old behaviors to resurface and believed I was strong enough to endure one night of pleasure hanging out with my old playmate's. It all came back: the drugs, gambling and the streets until I was doomed sinking in my sorrows of addiction and depression.

We create our own damage in our lives when we are not centered around the Lord. And there are 3 major points in life that we must have in order just to see the end of the tunnel and it's called the 3 (B)s -Balance- Boundaries and Beliefs. God gives us his grace and mercy to help us stay in alignment with the word and his commandments we must understand that with that gift we must keep our Balance in life not too much of this or that negative influence but strive to surround ourselves in God's protection and Boundaries that will keep us from being pushed out of the sight of the Lord for when we are not covered by the blood of Jesus Christ we can easily be backed into a corner and be unstable and Beliefs we must change our old ways of thinking so we can receive the word of God and his promises for the world is consumed with deception and lies but the renewal of our minds gives room for growth.

Damaged "But God"

Because I continue to find excuses for the streets Shy began to outgrow me and she realized that no matter how much she loved me if I didn't love myself enough to see what I was jeopardizing then she wasn't willing to risk her life and our sons trying to save me. After many years of tears and wishing for her dreams to come true reality set in and she realized that her dream was apparently there already—that someone to love her and someone she could love. That someone was Amir after almost dying giving birth to him she remembered what that felt like and she understood that she could never sacrifice their lives for myself destructive behavior. Our son was her soul mate and the one piece of me that no one could ever take away, not even me.

After working her butt off she got the promotion she worked hard for, for many years. She had a chance to relocate and did just that because she couldn't fix me but knew she had to take things in her own hands for Amir and herself so she moved to Pennsylvania the greatest move she could have ever done and I even believed in her mind that she hoped that one day I would get it together and put them first but she wasn't waiting around to see or find out and for real I believe that is what I hoped cause I knew Shy was done and nothing was ever going to change that period.

I went from all that a man could hope for and I mean a flush life. I had a trophy wife and a family that believed in me and who was willing to help me become great at whatever I desired and I gave it all away because of my poor decisions and seriously without God life is impossible to be happy.

I felt I was broken. Damaged and trapped in my self-pity I couldn't see beyond the rearview mirror for my life had become full of darkness. I went back to prison six times from 2001 to 2014 and because Shy took care of everything for me after she moved out of state I lost at least four apartments and became homeless and helpless. It appeared my sources of support were doing more work to assist me then I was doing for myself. Mentally I was so unstable I lost touch with myself. I tried to kill myself three different times by overdosing and what's so sad about that is once again I couldn't succeed in death correctly.

I checked myself into the Topeka Rescue Mission and cried every night for about a week until a friend said they got this program that would help me find some relief in my pain and hopefully help me find my way back to Christ Jesus. I knew in the past that God was available but I only used him when I was going through my life's struggles and at that moment I knew I needed him. I gave him a try once again and just like the last time and last time before that and the last time before that God showed me he could make me or break me. I got into the program and it gave me that balance and structure that Shy gave me and I began to see the hope for tomorrow. I exhaled in the program and used my spare time to get back into lifting weights—a passion I've always had and I became strong again mentally and physically and everyday because of the classes I attended I found myself back deep into a relationship with God. So once again I took off running but not in the race to succeed but the race of failure and again because I did as I always did—trying to prove to everyone that I was OK or for better word, untouchable.

I never told anyone I was at a mission because it was embarrassing so I had to keep up my fronts as if I was still with my family. It didn't matter because I knew when the lights went off I was still covered in darkness and sadness. Leaving the mission center many times to go gamble and hangout with my friends I found myself trapped in the heat of things literally one bad mistake after another and then the drugs came back in my moment of weakness to satisfy a losing night. For some reason I just couldn't overcome the addiction of self-gratification and it wasn't long after that I robbed a drug dealer and was forced to move out of Topeka, Kansas.

Damaged "But God"

I moved to Olathe, Kansas, to live with my youngest daughter's mom and I brought my behavior and baggage along with me. I had the chance to try to rebuild my life with my daughter Erin and we did spend some time together but I was still on bullshit and didn't take full advantage of the situation. One night after using cocaine I had a heart attack and was rushed to the hospital and when I got there I was told I had blocked valves to my heart and I needed to have a stent placed so the flow of blood could help operate my heart. What was it going to take for me to see I deserve to live. With all that I've been through and was going through I should have been dead but God had something planned and he was indeed building me up for it but I didn't see it yet I was still alive.

I needed help and my parole officer made it clear that if I didn't get it I was going back to prison so once released from the hospital I went to a half   house and got into a another drug program, that program also   s that dealt with mental health illnesses so I got involved. At   d like any other program just a lot of brain wash and the   uff but one day I was asked to leave cause I dosed off in   I left the case manager brought me to her office and ask me what's the purpose of you always trying when you clearly don't want to change. She said Charles you have been through many program treatments and seriously you could teach the course but my question is why do you keep coming back cause apparently with your record it's a proven fact that prison is much easier for you no accountability or responsibility for you to uphold just get your quick fix and clean up and hell you go right back to the insanity but why do you keep coming back??? I said because I don't want to die and I have seen the good in me I just don't know how to keep it as I started to cry she said I'm not going to do what has always been done to you I'm not going to kick you out nor am I going to force you to stay she said I want you to walk outside and as you open the door understand that you have a choice to reenter the center or you can leave and I won't call your parole officer but you need to find out what makes you keep coming back and for once know that the choice is yours.

I came back into the building and I went back to class and I understood from that moment on that being right could cost me everything and being wrong would cost nothing. Because of what I believed from learned behaviors I only had to prove that I didn't deserve to be great but if I just gave it a try and did succeed what would I lose. I was my worst critic and because I was willing to at least try I succeeded and completed the program 6 months of old information relearned and reprogrammed into my new way of thinking.

Damaged "But God"

That's when I met my Sunshine —a loving, sincere person who I just couldn't figure out. On our first encounter I stated how pretty she was and asked her for a kiss in the parking lot of a gas station and she looked at me so hard as if to say who the hell are you lol. Obviously I didn't get it so I continue to press on by saying what you too good to accept a complement and an offer to receive a kiss from me as if I was irresistible she shut her car door lol. But raised down her window and gave me her number. I called that night.

Sunshine was a single mom of three: Carissa, Jasarra, and Tamerra. They were very close to their mom. They were beautiful and were very active in every sport. At first our courtship was great and I can remember laying across her stomach and telling her about all my hang-ups and grief and misfortunes that made up my damaged life. I told her it haunts me from time to time but with help I was managing it. She made a decision at that moment that no matter what I go through in life she would be there for me as long as I kept it real. And let me say she kept her promise and there were really some rough times. My addiction and mental health issues caused so many problems that it would have taken a woman like her to help me get through it all and today I know it was But God.

Sunshine hung on time and time again and did not once let go of my hands. She knew I brought my damaged life into hers and no matter how much pain the damage caused she just kept praying and didn't let her spirits be broken. She saw something great in me and gave it her all to make sure I knew it.

Damaged "But God"

During the early days of our relationship we had like most couples our share of ups and downs. Before me coming into her life she spent most of her days and nights at home with her girls. She was the real soccer mom type that was dedicated to everything they did. She had her own child-care business for many years and was well off financially.

I can remember that at first, I had to sneak in and out so I wouldn't disturb the function and routine of her girls. I would park at the empty house next door, and most of the time, I would get lost trying to get to her house. Sunshine daughters were just as beautiful as ever and smart and off the top didn't trust me. On one occasion I came over while they were still up and when they saw me they looked at me as if I had just broke into their home and they watched my every move lol I guess I had a tattoo on my forehead stating I'm damaged goods.

I don't want to say they were spoiled, because they weren't, but one thing for sure—they didn't want anyone to interfere with what they called normal. Sunshine worked hard for everything she had and had gone through some struggles but she never let it stop her from providing for and supporting her family.

In 2016, when I met Sunshine my son Charles Jr. had been arrested for attempted capital murder and several other charges. I was really going through so much cause my heart was filled with guilt because I knew I had failed him as a father. Growing up Charles Jr only wanted to be with me and I can remember many times I would drop him off at daycare and or to school and by the time I got back to my car he would be standing beside me crying his little eyes out no daddy don't leave. Charles watched me close whenever I was around and once I took him with me to go gamble on the block and as I was betting he grabbed the dice and said 7 at the time it was funny even though I lost.

I remember having some of the best cars and even though I wasn't a drug dealer most of my cars fit that description of one and the one thing I made sure of when I would pick up Charles Jr was to make sure he was fascinated with all the perks and detail I put into them. Like I had a PlayStation installed in the glovebox with a pullout screen so he could always have something to do while I was driving lol. I realize I was far from winning the award for the perfect Dad but I was indeed the most creative Dad my son knew and as I would always pull up in a different car I never actually pulled up to educate him with the traumatic experience of being a street dude knowing that everything that glitters truly isn't gold.

Because his mother didn't have her own brothers around and all my brothers weren't in the picture as my kids grew up they seen a lot of role models that were in the streets and Charles Jr was like me always curious about how the streets made life look so glamorous not to mention he watched me with the car's jewelry and women and I really never thought it would consume him. I don't remember ever talking to Charles Jr about God and I'm sure all my behaviors and reactions to the streets showed him that life was sweeter being a thug wow if only I could have shown him how great God really is.

It was because of Sunshine and her support that I made it through his trial. To have a child subjected to so much at the age of sixteen was more than I could bear. I can only imagine what he was going through, and I can remember my days of loneliness and fear when I myself went through the same thing at his age.

Damaged "But God"

Because Sunshine spent so much time with me going back and forth to court for Charles Jr it added unwanted stress to her relationship with her daughters. No one truly knew what I was going through especially her daughters. All they knew was that their best friend was absent in their lives. Sunshine tried to be there for me so much that she started to miss games and normal family activities that later caused the girls to move in with their dad. In the blink of an eye she began to lose control of her home and girls.

The one thing I've learned about Sunshine is she always put herself in a position where she must become Superwoman in order to satisfy everyone and through her ambition to please and help everybody she gets overwhelmed and it always turns out that she is the problem but really she was the Hero but must of the time it went unnoticed.

Her girls were her world and the decision to allow them to go with their dad was bitter and sweet but mostly hurtful. She had never put anything in front of her babies. Her life was really upside down and very disturbing because she really wanted to please us all yet the only outcome was guilt and pain and blame. Her ex-husband got the girls and my son was found guilty and given a lot of time and my addiction went out of control and she slowly became numb to life because she felt she failed us all.

Damaged "But God"

I remember when we first got together I believed that my struggles were over because everything was going well I just completed the drug treatment and was getting help with my mental health issues and I was in a new relationship but as always there was something someone missing "God".

I was doing good but I didn't have the armored shield of the spirit around me so when Charles Jr situation hit me I had nothing to lean on and although Sunshine was there it was so easy to lose what I didn't have which was faith. Sunshine stepped in and made it bearable but without a power greater than my will I was surely headed down to what had always made me complete and whole "my addictions".

At the beginning we did everything together we took long walks to the lake and worked out together and Sunshine helped me to begin to enjoy life again. Sunshine would come to the halfway house with dinner and we would talk for hours on the phone. I remember when I was going out of town to see Amir in Pennsylvania it was going to be the first time I was going to be away from Sunshine and it was the first time I was going to see Shy and Amir in over a year. I was so excited and proud to be clean and in a good place in my life because when I seen Shy last I was not doing well at all.

Sunshine took me to the airport and I couldn't stop crying it felt like I would never see her again why I don't know but before I got out of the car I explained to her a thousand times like she was a kid. Make sure you pay attention to your surroundings, make sure you keep your phone on and charged and make sure you eat be careful and don't hesitate to call me if anything happens and most of all remember I love you.

When I got to Pennsylvania I had the time of my life. Me and Amir really enjoyed ourselves and it was really nice to see Shy and to know she was happy in a relationship it made me feel great cause she really did deserve to be happy and I could see she was and I won't lie I was a bit jealous lol but I guess that's normal especially when you realize you messed up in the first place. It was amazing how much Amir had grown and he had all his friends come meet me and we played basketball every day and what I didn't realize was Amir had a lot of my ways. I remember playing basketball with him and he got real competitive and got so upset that he threw the ball after I fouled him and I was wtf who is this kid lol but not just that he was real smooth with his conversation and all his friends young and older just gravitated to his every demands. I don't want to sound crazy but I never ever worried about Amir and his decision making cause I knew Shy and her family would surround him with the best support and direction that would keep him from following in my footsteps I just knew it.

I called Sunshine every morning and night to make sure she was still waiting on me lol and when it was time to leave Amir and Shy I really seen how tough my son was and I will forever see those big eyes full of tears that he tried hallelujah his best to fight off and even I turned my head so he wouldn't see me start to cry it was funny but sad we both did everything we could to show each other it was ok until we see each other again and poor Shy even she got caught up in our willingness to be strong for one another. That was the saddest moment in my life cause I realize he was stronger than me and before I got out of the car Amir said it's ok daddy I'll see you stop crying, my little man just like his mom always in the solution.

Damaged "But God"

Sunshine was there waiting for me at the airport and I've never been so happy but this was going to be a major fact in my life till this day that she would always be there waiting for me no matter what. After settling in we had to get ready for my son Charles Jr trial and after a long fight and many tears he was convicted and sentenced. Although I felt he was accused of crimes he didn't do I still felt that it was my fault cause I should have been there for him and I just wanted to hold him but just as I did many years before Charles Jr did not shed one tear he just turned to his mom and said I'm sorry I love you and as he looked at me he nodded his head and I felt his unspoken pain.

Once again I didn't cry out to God for comfort and I didn't reach out to the ones that loved me I went to the dark side of my grief and drowned myself in the feel good moments of isolation and drugs. I enter a place where my addiction got out of control and the gambling became an outlet to help me financially to stay in my insanity. Sunshine was being turned in so many ways. I overdosed twice in the same year and each time Sunshine was there to save my life. There was even a time when I shot myself while going after someone during a drug altercation and I didn't even know I had been shot. Because I wasn't taking care of the wound I got an infection in my big toe and had to get it amputated. During this time in my life everything seemed doomed and I completely gave up. Nothing mattered, and all my actions showed that it didn't. I robbed and stole to keep my addiction fed and no matter how hard Sunshine cried for her safety and love for me I just couldn't understand what I was doing because I stayed drugged out and my sense of reality was full of confusion and drama. I began to neglect Sunshine and many times failed to hear her cry of the fear for her life and also the pain of seeing me daily put my life in danger.

From the beginning she vowed to hold on regardless to what happened and I truly believe that she didn't expect a merry go round of nightmares and I must say today she is one hell of a woman who endured more than her share of reoccurring circumstances and unfortunate consequences. After I had been jailed on two separate drug cases she never left my side. Sunshine even put more work end then what my lawyer did on each of my cases and it was her dedication and ground work that brought me home and got both cases dismissed. And still that wasn't enough for me to see that God once again provided a way out of no way and that although I didn't acknowledge him he continue to stand in the gap of all my mess wow what a mighty God. And it's so crazy but even my lawyer told Sunshine she was blessed with some force that was even greater than his 30 years of practice, But God.

After getting released I had a stroke and a heart attack and one overdose after another. Sunshine stood strong and kept her faith until one day she couldn't take it anymore and had a mental break down. I used to watch her cry and always say, "Just stop Charles please Just Stop".

Sunshine went from having a perfect life enjoying the comfort of her girls and not knowing anything about the drug world and streets and most definitely was confused to see the great influence that addiction could have over someone. She was trapped inside a world that gave no mercy to her family and hopes for change it was slowly taking all her energy and she began to realize she had nowhere to turn nowhere to go and mentally and physically she just couldn't take it no more. The fight was killing her and she was watching me sink deeper into destruction and death.

Sunshine woke up one morning and she was going through all types of emotions but she knew she had to do something big in order to save her life and she reached out to her daughters the night before because she was having a mental break down and she needed her girls to rescue her. At the time I had no idea what she was planning and I watched her go in and out of the door several times and then the door closed for good and she was gone. I didn't know that her girls had come and gone with her because I was so busy getting high. I remember falling to sleep and was woke up by a knock at the door it was a new day I had slept for the entire day and there was no Sunshine no missed calls no nothing.

As I set there in my thoughts I realized Sunshine was gone for good enough. Enough of my foolishness she had had enough.

Damaged "But God"

As the next day began so did my urgency to get high and hopefully act as if everything was ok. I invited some friends to come over to watch the football game and maybe do some gambling. I had about 6 friends and my nephew come over and it was one of those nights where we did as we usually did everyone was just chilling when the door came open we were being robbed like something out of the movies and what was strange I didn't even see it coming cause normally high or not I am always aware of my surroundings but before I knew it guns were pulled and shots ranged from everywhere. Bullets we're going everywhere and I was in the middle and the one thing that mattered to me was that I had to make this stop. I didn't care about my life I just heard all the screaming and shouting and I wanted to help whoever I could hopefully save their lives. Before it was done and over I had witnessed a young man lose his life and two people injured and one fighting for her life. And as I panic I could only think where is my Sunshine omg.

With everything happening I was forced to watch the young man take his last breath and I ran to carry the woman out of the house I witness her fear as she said don't let me die. As the police and ambulance arrived I was immediately placed in cuffs and was escorted to the police station and was later arrested and put on a 48 hour hold but before I was transported to jail I had to heart attack and was rushed to the hospital. I remained in the hospital for three days and was then escorted to the county jail and booked for unrelated drug charges. When I was able to make my phone call I tried calling Sunshine no answer so then I tried my mom and daughter and was informed that Sunshine was aware of my situation but couldn't talk because she had checked herself into a mental hospital.

I didn't know what to do and for the first time in awhile I scared to death and like always when I'm in trouble I could hear myself crying God help me but afterwards immediately put my mask of survival mode on.

The charges of homicide was never charged to me but I was on hold by my parole officer until the ballistic was ran on the guns recovered from the scene and after the test proved I had nothing to do with the shooting I still had to stay in jail for drug charges.

During the 10 months fighting the charges Sunshine came back and went to our house to salvage whatever she could only to find out that our house was immediately broken into as so as I was taking to jail. She took what she could and left Kansas City Kansas as fast as she could and moved in with her sister in Belton Mo.

I can think back to the time when a friend asked Sunshine and I to go to church. We went to the Pentecostal Powerhouse Church, and the pastor, Donald Moore, said, "God hasn't given up on you." I see the flashback of that incident in our house and as everyone was running for survival I recall all the nightmares I had and still do have and it's amazing how God took Sunshine out of there before the madness came and not to mention I'm alive to tell the story. God had more for me and even though I stayed in my mess he wasn't through with me yet.

Damaged "But God"

Once released and getting the case down to a misdemeanor we joined Pentecostal Powerhouse Church, and Pastor Moore and the church became our family. I'm mentioning this because it's important to understand how at the right time and the right place God can put you in alignment with the spirit of a church family that accepts you for who you are and where you are in your journey to serve the Lord.

I can't say I wasn't challenged on my faith and desire to change cause I was and moving to Belton wasn't enough cause no matter where I went I was still having to deal with the baggage of my past and still there I was the center of all my problems.

We made a effort to stay grounded in the Lord and I understood Sunshine wasn't going for anything less than me getting myself together she made it clear she wasn't going to be uncomfortable nor unhappy anymore. I have to admit there were moments of weakness when I lost focus and only through the grace and mercy of the Lord was I able to regain my view of a better me which was more important than the struggles of my past. While in church one day Pastor Moore said out of nowhere, "Write the book Charlie". Write the book and tell the truth and watch God bless you cause nobody but God can hold you accountable for a better tomorrow in your life and let the word of God be your inspiration to your message.

I haven't always allowed God to use me for his purpose and the knowledge of the word wasn't always my first choice for direction yet through it all because of God's continuous love for me his loving hands surrounded me with his truth in my life and most definitely he has shown me some great miracles. Throughout all the trials and institutionalized behaviors that I have been faced with over the years I still do believe that my legacy is far from completion as I began to layer by layer unfold my true worth in this world and in God's plan.

Because of the many masks I had to cover up with so my emotions wouldn't be revealed those same masks began to trap me from reality. To be able to transform from one mask to another was beginning to be impossible, for I became lost in the characters so deep that I was no longer able to adjust but failed deeper into the false sense of my thoughts that allowed me to continue my institutionalized thinking and out of control drug abuse. I had to really search God and my heart so I could possibly become normal again and I knew I would have to make some drastic changes and the thing I had to do was truly surrender and let go and let God.

Damaged "But God"

As we tried to rebuild our lives, Sunshine and I knew we had a long hard road ahead of us with my addictions and fear to succeed causing us still more issues mainly because I have still yet to see and know what success would look like in me and I didn't realize it at the time but one of the things God showed me everyday was his face especially when he opened my eyes was that that in itself was a success.

By the time I came home Sunshine had reestablished her own relationship with the Lord and got involved with the church. As her faith in the Lord grew stronger so did her strength in our relationship. Just knowing Sunshine was putting God first in her life it helped me begin to balance out my own life and each decision I started to face became easier to understand and my choices were so much more grounded and my commitment was not just a filler but showed permanent results. And as time and change began to come and go it was apparent that in Sunshine 's house we were going to serve God. (Lol)

I don't want to mislead anyone with saying God said it was going to be easy and there will be no more problems and or pain and struggles cause that would be a lie. When Satan notice that God has your attention and he sees you winning and that hold he use to have has been replaced with God's promise to break the chains and the evidence of his grace and mercy shows in your life that's it well let me put it this way if you are not surrounded by the blood and the spirit at all times you can get relaxed and right then that's when Satan throws a hook and it can be just as simple as a phone call from an old playmate or dinner wasn't cooked on time by your spouse or the kids ate the last cereal, now stop and catch up to the patterns that in your past that caused you to just go off that's what happens when you leave just an inch of room for satan to confuse your thoughts. It happened to me I was still just trying to prove a point that I could get over my past and all I had to do was allow God to work to the point where I could pick myself up off the floor and after standing up, I could go back to normal or what I wanted to be normal.

Damaged "But God"

After all these years I was still challenging God. I was thinking after God fixed something in my life, I could control it without him after it was fixed and each time he showed me that the damage that had entrapped me and caused others to also fall into my madness was no match for him and all his power. I fell victim to many times to excuses of why? And all alone

God was showing me that if only I just stop he will continue to make his power known in my life I just needed to let him finish his work.

From an early age I noticed what my choices in decision making had caused me and how God held me up even when I didn't live up to his expectations he continue to show me that my trials weren't greater than his power. I still made excuses that because I came from a world full of damage it made me feel that it was easier to block out the noise of life and all it's expectations and I created a false sensation that would build up this sense of strength that years later I came to know as fear. And not until I witness and understood God's true grace did I understand how I for years I gave into the fear that caused the monster in me to wear the many masks that wasn't real and that in order to get released I must open up fully to God's mercy.

God can redirect all my destructive behaviors and turn my prayers into repentance that will hopefully show the good in me. I get up every morning accepting my faults while acknowledging my strength to become great in God's work. No matter how many times I've come short of my responsibility as a man, a father, and a husband, God proved to me that he had his hands in it all and regardless to how long it took me to get to this point it was all in his timing and with the help of Sunshine and her constant motivations for me to be the best me it gave me the courage to face that man in the mirror even though I didn't know how or what that man truly looked like because of the many masks that I used as protection to keep my (11) year old mind from developing. What's not so funny I'm still after all these years trying to grow up.

I was a people-pleasing kid only looking for acceptance. Even most of my friends believed I was this killer tough guy that had no fear but I was full of fear. If only they knew the character they faced was just a scared made-up individual that was trapped in this damaged fantasy hoping to be let out of the known and unknown fears.

This story is about Damaged "But God." My testimony about my life's journey and the journal of all my hopes and let downs that has caused so pain to others and myself. And how even in my mess God protected me, restored my family, created in me a clean spirit, healed my sickness, changed my blues to new, taught me to love myself, seen me through my trials. God performed the miracle that man said can't be done. God put a stronghold around the masks that have stopped me from being a child and a man. But God and all his mighty power can bring and has brought me to a new freedom.

Damaged "But God"

I can remember lying in the hospital bed many times wondering what I was going to tell my kids this time because of my near death experiences with overdose and suicidal mishaps. I had the constant question that I knew they would have and even I had why unfortunately I didn't make it home? I never had to explain it because the strong women behind me always had an excuse that would protect them from the truth. There were times I just had to give it to the Lord and count it all joy because I was so blessed time and time again when I should have been dead but God's grace and mercy kept me. In my criminal behaviors and my addictions and although I suffered mentally I always came back to life and reality. I've had many friends and just people in general who didn't survive the trauma of their relapses and are buried in prison because of their criminal activities and literally zoned out in their mental illness But God had unfinished work that he was doing in me.

As I said earlier I challenged God because I always believed it should have been me to die and not Carl and I kept my foot on my own neck hoping that God would release me from my duties of life yet no matter what I did and how hard I tried God showed me that it wasn't my time and he (God) could do it again and again—the impossible.

Being stabbed ten times and being the only one able to walk away was not by my will and power but by the grace of God. I tried many times to die, and God just wasn't ready to open the gates of heaven to me yet. And I've done so much wrong and still God favored me. His mercy and grace is not hard to see. For my mother taught me at a young age that God can and is willing to keep me for his purpose "repentance" is the key. There was a time when I would black out lost in my mental health illness of blackness and would walk around trying to find my way to Carl. It was beyond my knowledge of what I was doing out of control in the cold sitting on the porches of stranger's houses for four to five hours with nothing on more than summer clothes in the winter, and someone would notice me not knowing who I was but would bring me into their home to keep me warm and when I came through I wouldn't know where I was or how I got there.

God has seen me through some really tough times. I've been on parole for 26 years and I'm waiting now on a decision that would allow me to be discharged and all I can say is But God cause it's been so long for a reason and I'm alive today because of being on parole I managed to be accountable in some odd ways by using parole as a clutch when I can't get it right rather it be in life mentally and physically prison revolving door has been the solitary to my solution to get back on track and I know it's crazy but at the time it was all I could lean on. So I believed!

My story is far from over by writing this book it helped me released my guilt and pain that I felt was the cause of all the damaged that I believed was in my life and once I truly took a look at all my actions I began to see how many lives I affected. And my hope is that one day my victims and even my family may be able to forgive me and see what the world and satan wanted for my life was death and fear but God turned it around and made it for his purpose. I still have nightmares of all the damage that I endured and that I caused in other people lives yet I pray that my testimony becomes a reality check to those who are still suffering and that they understand that it's never too late to open your hearts and except what God has always meant for your life. To travel in life trapped by the many masked deceptions that you have created to protect your true worth is insanity and until you see by searching the word of what God's grace and mercy have and has always been directed to perform in your life you won't understand its great work that is in you. It took many years for me to see that all along God had a plan for me his presence was evident in my journey from day one yet I choose to allow my will to be fulfilled and I never enjoyed a moment of peace but when I let go and let God peace surrounded me and I felt the presence of the Lord.

Pastor Donald Moore the book of life is as you preach daily it's our pressing on that's what matters to the Lord for he gives us great instructions a manuscript of how to endure and its in the Bible. He also promised that his grace and mercy will never leave us. I thank you for your patience and commitment and most definitely your direction on what the word of God says. You always say it's in the word lol and I've found peace in the word of God.

To each one of my children and especially their Mother's in this journey that I have traveled your lives were truly challenged and I've been the leader of all the madness and in my worst moments of isolation and fear I only have God to thank for you cause through it all you have always made me out to be better than I deserve to be recognized. I thank you for all for your patience and I appreciate all that you do. I'm so sorry it took me so long to get it and I never meant to cause you so much pain. I'm better today because you never gave up on me and if I never said it my story would not be a testimony without all your prayers and truly your presence.

To Sunshine a new chapter is created daily and I'm so thankful that God made you just for me. We all have been changed and experienced some dramatic things that only God could have brought us through. You would always say just stop Charles please just stop, I want you to know that whenever I have a moment of despair I not only hear your voice but I also see your tears and I know your worth and as long as God is the center of my life you'll never have to make that plead again. For sure I wouldn't have gotten this far without you. We only needed one good break to turn our entire life around and to God be the glory we have had many lol.

To my family especially my Mom thank you for giving it your all in everything you did for me. We came through the jungle but like any mama bear you stayed with me through it all. There will never be a complete book of what you mean to me cause it's not enough words to express it. Thank you for being a Mother to my brothers and sister and me. You are the inspiration to my story and the sacrifices you have made to us all is truly appreciated. I love you Gerald-Baby.

And last to my kids I can't change the past and surely I've made lots of mistakes and excuses because of my absence but I pray that you all can forgive me and except me for where I am today and just know God is not done with us yet. I love you Hopie, Faith, Erin, Charles Jr and Amir and

I'm proud of you all. Even though I just discovered that I had a son that I never knew about until recently. 10 years of no knowledge from the top of my voice I say Thank you God for allowing me to be clean and filled with the spirit to be everything and more to my son Royce. This is the beginning of the best chapter in my life with God all things are possible. And I just must say Royce you came at the right time for daddy is in the right place to be everything you need HALLELUJAH.

In life we go through a great many challenges we get lost in our ways and views and choose the ugly over the good, and even hurt the ones we love just to find reasons for our own emotions. It's called damage and the results of those feelings leave scars and unexplainable behaviors that we mask to stop the pain of the monster of our fears and grief and all the mental health issues that haunt our existence. Fighting with no strength yet depending on God as we hold on we see his unchanging hand in the middle of our reality and the journey that takes a lifetime seems unbearable but we must believe that we can do things through Christ Jesus that strengthens us.

I must say that after all these years it's appropriate to announce that my life wasn't damaged from my experiences or my expectations but was filled with a plan that God saw through for his purpose. Although I didn't see it at the time God was waiting on me to surrender and lean on him. To truly have repentance and show it by allowing his will and my willingness to follow before he literally took control and when he did God gave me the words to my testimony so my story could be an example of his greatness and power that has surely made me over .

Damaged "But God"

Change
Just the other day, as I reminisce back to the lovely night of my arrival,
I never knew I would be faced to learn the skills of survival.
Growing up in a world full of drama yet destined for fatal destruction,
I always imagine myself way up in the clouds protected from corruption.
Over and over again I see these pictures of many unshaped faces,

Never focusing on the images or the objects in strange places.

Here I am separated from life and all its games,

Thinking to myself what has caused my life to change.

Prison bars and one high that leads to a greater high I can't help myself I'm lost in my addiction,

Confused, scared, trapped, Oh Lord, why is this to be my conviction?

I'm day dreaming it could possibly be the road that was paved for me "Change"

The direction that gave me no direction "Change"

The dream of many broken desires "Change"

Facing the mirror of my yesterday I believe in my heart that today I live not to repeat,

But my quest is to understand my fears and let the Lord guide my sight and protect my feet.

Change

Words of encouragement:

I lived my life and every word is true. I faced death many times and watched it surround me like a storm. I also seen and heard the cries of many men and women who had no hope for tomorrow because they were trapped by their prison walls rather it was mental illness, addiction and or suicidal behaviors either way I watched them lose sight of the truth. In my own journey for over 40 years I believed my life to be damaged and unrepairable yet the answer and solution to my problems was there all along right in my reach all I had to do was surrender but I was blinded by what I believed controlled me. The masks of protection from the fears of life not being accepted and the need to be feared in order to prevent emotions. Running from God's grace and mercy 40 years only to understand that what God gave me I couldn't find from anything else nor no one.

Damaged "But God"

Recognizing Achievable Conscious Emotions
Charles Dean Bowser
Cdbowser65@gmail.com

Damaged "But God"

Charles Dean Bowser

Damaged "But God"

Charles Dean Bowser

Damaged "But God"

Charles Dean Bowser

Damaged "But God"

Charles Dean Bowser

Damaged "But God"

Charles Dean Bowser

Damaged "But God"

Charles Dean Bowser

Damaged "But God"

Charles Dean Bowser

Printed in the USA
CPSIA information can be obtained
at www.ICGtesting.com
LVHW090113160923
758231LV00006B/188

9 798888 102305